brilliant

customer
service

Debra Stevens

Prentice Hall
is an imprint of

Harlow, England • London • New York • Boston • San Francisco • Toronto • Sydney • Singapore • Hong Kong
Tokyo • Seoul • Taipei • New Delhi • Cape Town • Madrid • Mexico City • Amsterdam • Munich • Paris • Milan

© Pearson Education Limited 2010

The right of Debra Stevens to be identified as author of this work has been asserted by her in accordance with the Copyright, Designs and Patents Act 1988.

Pearson Education is not responsible for the content of third party Internet sites.

ISBN: 978-0-273-73807-7

British Library Cataloguing-in-Publication Data
A catalogue record for this book is available from the British Library

Library of Congress Cataloging-in-Publication Data
Stevens, Debra.
    Brilliant customer service / Debra Stevens.
        p. cm.
    Includes bibliographical references and index.
    ISBN 978-0-273-73807-7 (pbk. : alk. paper) 1. Customer relations.
2. Customer services. I. Title.
    HF5415.5.S7376 2010
    658.8'12--dc22

                                                                2010033868

10 9 8 7 6 5 4 3 2 1
14 13 12 11 10

Typeset in Plantin Regular 10/14pt by 3
Printed by Henry Ling Limited, at the Dorset Press, Dorchester, DT1 1HD

I dedicate this book to all my customers; they have taught me more about brilliant customer service than any books I have read or research I have done. I have learned from their example, and their high expectations have resulted in me having to raise my game. Without my customers I wouldn't have written this book.

And to my beautiful daughter Emily.

Contents

About the author

Debra Stevens is a successful trainer and speaker with over 15 years' experience of training people at all levels to improve their customers' experience. She is the founder of Sold Out Trainers, a highly successful experiential training company specialising in facilitating behavioural change in all aspects of dealings with people whether in customer service, sales, management or with colleagues and team mates. Debra has run her own successful small business for 14 years using the principles of *Brilliant Customer Service* to create successful partnerships with companies such as Royal Caribbean Cruise Lines, Penguin Books, Carlsberg, Coke and The Royal Bank of Scotland.

Debra would love to hear from readers with any comments, feedback and especially examples of where the principles in this book have made a real difference. To contact her email: debra@soldout-trainers.com.

Acknowledgements

I would like to thank;

- My husband Pete Rice for all his support and his endless patience with proof reading.

- My son Drew for saying just the right words of encouragement when I needed them most.

- My daughter Lizzie for looking after me on my final week of writing.

- My mentor Mark Short for his straight talking and wonderful support.

- Michael and Christine Heppell without whose help I would not have got this opportunity.

I would also like to thank Alejandra Friess, Deputy Manager of Las Iguanas, Milton Keynes; my hairdresser, Jo, from Zig Zag; Amazon; Stena Line; Disney and Steljes for their excellent customer service used as examples in this book.

Introduction

People expect good service but few are willing to give it.
Robert Gately (President, Gately Consulting)

I have found over the past 15 years of delivering customer services training at all levels, that the principles of brilliant customer service are very obvious. There is nothing complicated about it; there are no real mind-blowing theories; there aren't any brand new, exciting models. We know it all because we are customers and we know how we think and feel and what we want. We need to keep in mind, while reading this book, why it's so important – it's a cliché, but customers pay our wages.

If you are a business owner reading this, you will probably already be only too aware that to grow your business and make more money you need to keep your customers and get new ones, and the really great thing about delivering brilliant service is that it does both of these things. There is nothing more satisfying than getting new business from a recommendation and when they turn into an advocate they also recommend you; it really is a snowball effect. If you work in a customer services department on the front line, or you serve customers in the retail or entertainment industry or maybe you work in travel, then your motivation for reading this book will be different. The statement that customers pay your wages is still true but for you this book will help your job become easier and more enjoyable. I hope it will help you to view customers in a different light. If you manage people on the front line, then use this book to help train and empower them; one of the great things about working in customer service is that the results are tangible and it can really get you noticed.

Five reasons why it is important to keep customers

1 Keeping customers, especially our best customers, allows us to earn back the money it cost to get them in the first place. The longer we keep them, the more our original investment pays off.

2 Happy customers are more likely to buy more from us. They are easier to sell to; they are more likely to listen to our sales story and read our marketing or respond to an advert because they already understand our offering and trust it.

3 Loyal customers are less likely to question the cost of our services and products because they have peace of mind to know we won't rip them off and will look after them when they have a problem. So loyal customers will pay more.

4 Experienced customers actually make our job easier because they know us and how we work; they are less likely to need their hand holding. They tend to make fewer calls to customer services or fewer visits, so generally they cost less to service.

5 The most important one of all: if your existing customers recommend you, you get new customers for free with no marketing, advertising or intensive sales campaigns. They will also come to you with a receptive frame of mind because they have had a recommendation.

The challenge

How we are treated as customers and how we treat our customers can have such a major effect on the quality of some of our most enjoyable experiences. Holidays can be made or broken based on how we are looked after. Travel can be incredible or terrible based on how we are left feeling after the experience. Trips to the shops, nights in restaurants, buying a new car and browsing the Internet can either leave us feeling valued and appreciated or frustrated and neglected. How much energy do we use in getting upset about poor service and how does it really impact our feelings about the companies we engage with? Would you pay more for brilliant service?

We are all customers and we all experience customer service several times every day. We are aware of when we are really 'wowed' and when we are left feeling unimpressed, so why is it that when we deal with customers ourselves we don't always deliver the 'wow'? In terms of knowledge and experience, it is one area we should be experts in because we know what works based on our own experiences and we get those by the thousands every year. The challenge is when an example of poor customer service affects us, we feel the effect and we have an emotional response. When we deliver poor service to someone else, we can be blinded to its effects, we don't feel the emotion and we fail to truly empathise with our customer. Brilliant customer service is all about emotion and how we make our customers feel. The first thing we have to do is acknowledge that it does not necessarily come naturally to us – it does take commitment and hard work.

When was the last time you were truly impressed with the service you received? It might be difficult to remember because we are much harder to please as customers than ever before. We are used to everything coming fast; it's a very immediate society, and expectations are higher than ever. I remember putting my car in for a service 10 years ago and it coming back valeted. I was delighted. Now it is totally expected; it has become normal, definitely a neutral experience. If we want to create a 'wow' now, we have to do something unexpected, something that creates a positive emotional response in our customer. Ironically, because we now communicate so much using modern technology we can be wowed with great listening, with empathy, with a genuine smile and a real human response. So if someone were to ring me and tell me my car needed a service in a warm and engaging way, help me book it in and then remember me when I went to the desk to hand over the keys, I would be wowed because that has never happened to me. Normally, I am ignored at the desk; I get no eye contact or connection and they compensate for that by valeting my car! What does this mean? It means that so many times we can create a wow which costs absolutely nothing except some commitment from us or our staff to treat our customers as humans.

The good news

The good news is that with some simple tools and techniques everyone can create wow moments for their customers. The main focus of all my customer service training has always been the people skills, and this book takes the best from the training I have delivered and learned over the past 15 years. It is simple and practical and the skills and techniques are applied and make a real difference straight away.

Why be brilliant?

The obvious answer to this is if you aren't, someone else will be and you will lose customers and ultimately money. Of course, this is true but giving brilliant customer service has other key benefits:

● **Morale and motivation**. What we often forget is that when our customers have a positive emotional response to something we do, we also get a positive emotional response ourselves. Delivering brilliant service makes us feel as good as the customers. Often we are rewarded by appreciation from the customer; appreciation actually raises our levels of serotonin (a neuro chemical produced in the brain) so it makes us feel physically better. Thirty minutes of appreciation gives us as much serotonin as 30 minutes of vigorous exercise!

● **Team spirit**. Giving brilliant service to our external and internal customers creates a positive environment which can be pleasant and fun to work in. Staff turnover is reduced and commitment is higher. Whether you manage or are part of a team, you can influence and inspire others if you lead the way by giving everyone you deal with a positive emotional response. Some of the best service I have ever had has been on cruise ships and the crew are the happiest bunch of people you could wish to meet, yet they work very long hours, deal with people with differing expectations and needs from all over the world; it's just infectious.

● **Enhanced reputation**. It's clear that if a company is known for its brilliant service, it will have a better reputation and be more likely to be held up as an example or receive positive publicity, but it's just as important for the customer-facing individual or manager in a customer service team. People who are recognised for giving brilliant service earn more money, get more promotions, win more prizes and get noticed. Why? Because they are still hard to find and happy customers equals more profit for any business. Anyone can get noticed if they commit to giving all their customers a positive experience.

● **Fewer complaints, less stress**. Upset and angry customers create stress for everyone. It is important to encourage customers to give feedback but they should never

have to complain about the way they have been treated.
Keep complaints down by always treating customers well.

Getting the most from this book

The first big question you need to answer is, 'Who are my customers?' and following on from that, 'Do I want to be customer service focused?' In the current economic climate the trend to stay in business has been to cut prices; on the high street it has become a buyers' market; it is incredibly competitive. Walking into a well known, high-street store recently to buy some cheap and cheerful holiday clothes, I was delighted to find several special offers and a value range, all of reasonable quality. With my arms full of clothes I went to the payment desk (being in a hurry I didn't want to try them on) only to find a queue at least 10 deep, with only one assistant on the till. Glancing around the store I noticed several members of staff merchandising and tidying up, completely oblivious to the queue of people. I waited five minutes, the queue barely moving, and like any other sensible person I dumped the clothes and went into another nearby store with similar special offers and good-value products. The most annoying thing was that as I left another member of staff asked me if I wanted to apply for a store card! This is a great example of a company that has completely forgotten who its customers are and is totally focused on product and not service. The point being, we have so much choice and even if we buy on price we still prefer efficient, speedy, brilliant service. This book will encourage you to re-focus on the customer and see things through their eyes; it's important to be open to what you see.

Although we refer to external customers a lot throughout the book, it is important to remember that not all of our customers are external; every company large or small has internal customers. They can be anyone you give a service to; for example, if you are in human resources or IT, everyone in your business is a customer. Internal customers are equally as important as external ones and often they are not treated equally. It's easy to become complacent with our internal customers and not be aware of the impact we are having because they are more familiar and our perception is that they are not as important. Giving our internal customers brilliant service has a positive effect on everyone including our external customers!

I have an office full of business and self-development books. Some are like old friends, consulted often, and have made a real difference to the way I live and work; others, if I am honest, have not been opened past the first couple of pages and others have been read and forgotten. This book is simple and practical because that is how I deliver my training; everything has been tried and tested and makes a difference. If you want to get noticed for your brilliant service, remember don't just read but DO! Reading a book has never changed anyone's life; putting into practice what you read does. It takes 30 days to make something a habit, so do the exercises until they are a habit. Funnily enough, you won't just become brilliant at customer service, but you will also become a brilliant people person, which will improve all aspects of your life.

CHAPTER 1

Customers
have changed

Customers have changed because the world has changed and it is constantly changing. Admittedly, I am getting old but I remember going to shops when the pace of life was so much slower; it seemed that people had more time and you were known by your name. There was time for a chat and relationships were stronger. We had less choice and the only way we could buy was through people either face to face or on the phone. Now there are large call centres to buy from; shopping centres full of large chain stores have replaced the local high street, and supermarkets selling everything you need seem to be everywhere. To top it all, we can buy anything 24 hours a day on the Internet without speaking to anyone.

Even the way we judge a first impression is different now:

- In the 1980s and 1990s, NLP authors claimed you only had 90 seconds to make a first impression.

- By the time the new millennium arrived, you only had four to seven seconds, according to hundreds of articles.

- In 2005, Malcom Gladwell's bestselling book *Blink* explained that people made first impressions in TWO seconds.

- And now a recent article from the BBC quotes a study which explains that Internet surfers form an impression 'in one twentieth of a second of viewing a webpage'.

Because of technology and the Internet we now have the potential to access instantly information that previously took weeks to obtain, so our buying decisions can be more complicated and confusing. Also, because we are constantly being bombarded by companies advertising their products wherever we go, we are more cynical and less trusting. We are also more independent and not so reliant on people to give us information, serve or sell to us; if we want to we can cut out any interaction with people completely. I remember that it was almost tradition to go into a travel agent in between Christmas and New Year to book the annual holiday. This experience meant sitting with an agent while they went through the options for you and could take up to an hour. Now you can have access to all of the travel companies with destinations all over the world and you can choose and book a holiday in less than five minutes while in your dressing gown.

In some ways this is all fantastic but as businesses we need to look at how we can make the most of any personal contact with our customers and when they are using technology. We must not take for granted the fact that they are also having an emotional experience which affects their perception of our business and whether they buy from us again or not. More importantly, are they damaging our reputation by spreading bad news or recommending us to others? Just as technology gives our customers access to millions of companies, it also gives them the ability to spread any bad or good news a lot further.

All of this means we have to work harder to build trust and loyalty; it doesn't come from serving the customers every day and building up friendships. A customer can now switch from one product or service to another without much cost either monetarily or emotionally. We can't take loyalty for granted because there is too

we can't take loyalty for granted because there is too much competition much competition; this is why we need to see every touch point with a customer as an opportunity in whatever medium.

Also, we now have the possibility to be accessible to many different types of customers with various life styles. Our customers can be all ages from all over the world with different needs and perceptions. We need to be more sensitive to diversity and we live in a world which can be a minefield of political correctness. It is not difficult to lose the goodwill and loyalty of one type of customer with the wrong marketing message or advert or something put on YouTube about yourself. Customers are fickle – you can be flavour of the month one minute and totally out of favour the next.

Customers still want you

Despite all of these changes, customers still want the same things they always did; it's just they now have different ways of getting them and a lot more choice if they don't get what they want. Customers still want a positive experience when they buy or use a service. They still have an emotional reaction with every interaction they have with a business even if it is on the Internet. There are still lots of customers who enjoy the personal experience of going shopping, even if they do all their research on the Internet. We still like to eat out, stay in hotels, go on holiday, visit attractions. Call centres are still growing and doing more business than ever dealing with customer enquiries on the phone. So the important thing is that we look at all of the contact we have with our customers and make sure it is brilliant.

> customers still want a positive experience when they buy or use a service

What do customers really want today?

- Information on products and services that's easy to get, relevant and helps them make the right decision. This can be well informed and available staff or it can be a well designed, easy to navigate website.

- To be treated well and have a positive experience. This could be human contact, a personal email, recorded message or an automated response system. If the experience is virtual, it should still make us feel supported and valued.

- Good value and peace of mind that they are not wasting their money. Reassurance that there is some way they can have any issues or problems dealt with minimises the risk of purchase and encourages customers to buy.

- The business transaction should be easy to do and make us feel good. It doesn't matter how they decide to do business with you, if it is too hard, takes too long and irritates them, they will go somewhere else.

- Once they have made a buying decision, customers want to receive their purchase straight away or as quickly as possible. Customers are not used to waiting for anything and will simply go somewhere else to get it.

- Someone at hand to give help if they need it.

brilliant tip

Think about how your customers have changed in the way they deal with you. Is their experience of doing business with you positive throughout? Identify areas that might need development and seek feedback from your front-line staff and the customers themselves.

Although customers have changed, their needs haven't: they still want the same things from us; they are just harder to impress and less likely to be loyal. This gives us a fantastic opportunity to be different and in an impersonal world we can really put the wow back into customer service.

brilliant recap

- Customers have changed because the world is so much faster paced and less personal.

- Customers want things more quickly and easily to reflect changes in the world.

- Customers are more independent and likely to seek out information about products and services. They are often more informed than we are about what is available to them.

- Customer loyalty is much harder to get and keep because of the amount of competition there is and the customers' easy access to it through the Internet.

- Customers still want the same things they always did and in this impersonal world we can have a real impact if we give customers brilliant personal service.

CHAPTER 2

The cornerstones of brilliant customer service

This chapter is all about the key people skills required for brilliant customer service. Whether you are on the front line dealing with customers or managing people who are, these fundamental skills are essential for all aspects of customer interaction, giving and creating more wow experiences that will keep them coming back with confidence and to recommend you to others. The same skills are used to connect with customers, to deal with customer complaints, build rapport and loyalty as well as selling more. These soft skills will be referred to throughout this book as they form the foundation from which everything else is built.

Why customers leave

What is the main reason customers defect? Would you say it is because they prefer someone else's product or are seduced by an advert or a special offer? Or is it because they didn't like our product or had problems with it? Actually it is none of these! The right answer is that a staggering 68% of customers defect because of the way they have been treated by a member of staff! (See Figure 2.1.) Also it can cost five times more to buy new customers as keep existing ones happy.

This means, it's people that lose customers because they treated the customers badly in some way. The great thing is most of us want to be nice and want to be liked and appreciated; we just

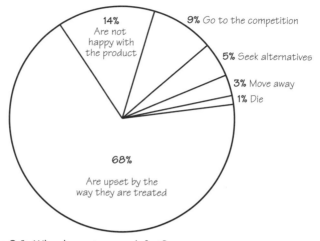

Figure 2.1 Why do customers defect?

need to be more aware of our impact. I have included tools and tips in this chapter which can make an amazing difference to the customer experience. They are easy to use and for the most part free. Firstly, we need to look at our attitude towards our customers and our perception of how they behave.

The customer really is king!

The greatest discovery of my generation is that human beings can alter their lives by altering their attitude of mind.

William James (Psychologist)

The first thing is to be honest with yourself about what you think of your customers. Imagine that you are seeing the customer through different coloured filters and that this affects the way you want to treat them. Do you see them as difficult and hard to please? Do you think they lie and are out to get whatever they can from you? (Grey filter) Perhaps you believe they are fickle and disloyal and don't really value you at all? (Grey filter) Or maybe even that they are stupid or don't care? (Grey filter) Or do you value and appreciate their contribution to your business and the paying of your wages? (White filter) The way we perceive our customers has huge impact on our ability to deliver brilliant service. As I mentioned in the introduction, delivering brilliant service should be easy and common sense; we talk about it all the time in our jobs and businesses. Some companies even hold huge conferences having it as the main theme, employing experts to speak on it, creating mission statements, committing to service excellence and yet it still doesn't happen, usually because neither they nor their employees really believe in it.

brilliant example

Some of you may remember the infamous quote from Gerald Ratner:

> Ratner's has got very little to do with quality ... I say because it's total crap.
>
> Gerald Ratner, former CEO of Ratner's Jewellers

This quote was picked up by a major national UK newspaper when he was asked, 'Aren't you making fun of your customers?' The next day the newspaper ran with the headline 'You 22-carat gold mugs'.

This is a perfect example of how customers can react, being portrayed as undervalued and stupid; the effect was dramatic on this large, successful business.

It's easy to fall into the trap of being negative about customers especially when we have to deal with difficult situations or what we see as unreasonable behaviour. The benefit of changing this attitude is that we not only deal with our customers with more empathy but we also feel better about ourselves. Try the following ideas on how to reframe your attitude.

The customer is stupid	The customer doesn't understand
The customer wants to rip us off	The customer wants the best value

The customer is demanding	The customer is important
The customer is always complaining	The customer is giving us feedback
The customer is irritating	The customers are all different
The customer is a nuisance	The customer pays our wages

☀ brilliant tip

Really be truthful with yourself about which filter you are looking at your customers through. Write down key words that represent how you really perceive the customer, and be aware of yourself when dealing with them. What are your expectations? How do you think they will behave? Do you find yourself getting exactly what you expected? Now look at ways to change your perception; start to see your customers in a new light through a different filter. Write a list of positive aspects about them. Why are they important? Why should you appreciate them? etc. and remind yourself all the time when dealing with them; be aware of how they still live up to your expectations. Make it part of your own personal or company policy to never speak badly of customers and to always have a positive perception.

It's hard to accept that we are responsible for how our customers behave, just by the way we think about them, but if we don't, we will never deliver the brilliant service we say we want. If we recognise our attitude and focus on our own behaviour, then we can often be rewarded by a more positive response, even when dealing with difficult situations. It is easy to blame others, when things don't go well and we can only work on ourselves, we cannot influence the behaviour of anyone, except

we are responsible for how our customers behave

through our own behaviour. Remember you can always choose your response to any situation or person.

brilliant definition

Responsibility

Response … ability – the ability to choose your response.

How do customers really want to be treated?

The following list will come as no surprise to anyone but as with all soft skills, they are hard to deliver well and consistently. Customers want:

- **To be listened to**. We all want to have our say and to feel that we are interesting.

- **To be understood**. Use effective questioning and clarifying skills to find out their needs or get to the bottom of a problem quickly as well as showing you care.

- **Genuine empathy**. This is so often missing and then the interaction might be efficient but it is cold leaving the customer feeling unappreciated.

- **Appropriate connection**. Our human impact is often what is remembered or makes for a great wow moment, but it does need to be appropriate to the situation and the type of customer.

- **To feel important**. Everyone thinks they are the most important person and if our customers are made to feel fantastic by us that's because they are!

- **Enthusiasm**. This goes back to our attitude and perception; a customer knows very quickly if you are negative or lethargic when dealing with them.

- **Flexibility**. Customers are individuals and have individual needs and they want to be treated as such, there is no size fits all.

The thin thread of connection

Whether you are dealing with customers face to face or on the telephone, it's important to make an appropriate connection. This often starts with eye contact and a warm smile. It's the same with the phone, except the smile is in the voice and the eye contact is your total commitment to focus on them without giving in to distractions.

Making the connection

To establish a connection you need eye contact and a smile ... easy! It can't be, because in my experience eye contact is one of the hardest things to achieve when you are being served. Next time you are in a motorway service station buying a cup of coffee or a magazine and filling your car with petrol, be aware of the eye contact or, in most cases, the lack of it. I play the game 'What do I have to do to get eye contact?' When you do get a wonderful smile and real eye contact, be aware of the effect it has on you; it's almost magical. My daughter, like a lot of teenagers, worked in a department store on a Saturday to earn some extra cash. I once went to meet her for lunch and as I was a bit early I thought I would do a bit of harmless spying on her. I found the till she was working on and hid behind a wall of china. I was delighted to see her greeting every customer with a warm smile and full eye contact. The effect on the customers was remarkable: they engaged in conversation with her; they smiled back and they left the till looking brighter and, dare I say it, happier. Even the grumpiest looking person in the queue could not escape my enchanting daughter. I thought at that moment I had a lot to learn from her. When I asked about it afterwards she said it made her day go faster and the job more enjoyable if she gave this little bit of herself. She also said that she found that most customers were really nice and interesting; her attitude was also right.

Once you have the connection, imagine a thin thread connecting you to the customer; it gets stronger the longer you hold it and it's always easy to break. The key is to be aware of the thread and work at maintaining it.

Are you listening?

The most basic of all human needs is the need to understand and be understood. The best way to understand people is to listen to them.

Ralph Nichols

The questionnaire below will help to evaluate your listening skills. Be honest with yourself or ask someone who knows you well to help, so it becomes a valuable awareness tool.

How do you rate as a listener?

Rate yourself (or have a friend help you) using the following scale:

5 = Always

4 = Almost always

3 = Sometimes

2 = Rarely

1 = Never

1 I allow the speaker to finish expressing themselves without interrupting.   ____

2 I actively try to develop my ability to retain important information.   ____

3 In a meeting or important phone conversation, I write down the most important details of a message.   ____

4 I avoid becoming defensive or excited if a speaker's views differ from mine.   ____

5 I repeat the essential details of a conversation back to the speaker to confirm that I have understood correctly. ____

6 I exercise tact in keeping the speaker on track. ____

7 I tune out distractions when listening. ____

8 I make an effort to show interest in the other person's conversation. ____

9 I understand that I'm learning little when I'm talking (I talk too much, listen too little?). ____

10 I sound as if I'm listening (I use paraphrasing, ask questions, etc.). ____

11 I remember that people are less defensive when they feel they're being understood. ____

12 I understand that I don't have to agree with the speaker. ____

13 In face-to-face conversation, I look for non-verbal forms of communication, such as body language, tone of voice and other signals which provide information in addition to the speaker's words. ____

14 I look as if I'm listening in face-to-face meetings (I lean forward, give eye contact, etc.). ____

15 I ask for the spelling of names and places when I'm taking a message. ____

Scoring how you rate as a listener

Rate yourself as follows:

64 or more = You're an excellent listener!
50–63   = You're better than average.
40–49   = You require improvement.
39 or less = You're not an effective listener. You need more practice!

To maintain the thin thread of connection, listening is vital. If a customer believes you are not listening, even for a couple of seconds, the connection will be lost. It's the same whether on the phone or face to face. The questionnaire above will help you highlight areas to work on. You should also be aware of your barriers to focused listening. If you can identify these barriers, you can bring yourself on track quicker and avoid breaking the connection.

brilliant tip

If you're finding it particularly difficult to concentrate on what someone is saying, try repeating their words mentally as they say it – this will reinforce their message and help you control mind drift.

Barriers to listening

- **Pre-empting**. Listeners evaluate the message before the customer has finished. In doing so they may change the message to fit what they thought it may be.

- **Flare up**. Listeners find difficulty in understanding exactly what the customer is saying; they focus on trying to make sense of it.

- **Distractions**. Interruptions, telephone calls and any sort of noise all disrupt the flow of communication.

- **Preoccupation**. Listeners are preoccupied with other issues and cannot concentrate on what the customer is saying.

- **Prejudice**. Listeners have prejudged the issues being discussed or the customer. They are only receptive to anything the speaker may say which will support their own prejudices.

- **Anxiety**. Listeners are worried about what is being said or what they are going to say.

- **Indifference**. Listeners are not interested in what the customer is saying and make no effort to sift out what might be useful and to hunt for clues.

● **Mental rehearsal.** Listeners are rehearsing what they are going to say next or thinking about what questions to ask. This could also be about jumping to solutions too quickly.

● **Replying.** Listeners are too busy thinking of what they are going to say in reply.

● **Assumptions.** Listeners assume they know what has been said.

● **Associations.** Listeners associate with the customer too much and they start to relive their own memories and experiences in their head.

The best way to deal with the above barriers is to practise 'focused listening'.

brilliant definition

Focused listening

Following the agenda of the customer, we must not be influenced by our own ego/beliefs, assumptions or judgements. Instead we need to ask relevant clarifying questions to find out more details and confirm our understanding of the customer. It's important to summarise and reflect back our understanding.

The art of focused listening

The following techniques include some of the most important cornerstones of brilliant customer service. Practise and perfect these skills as they will help you to create fantastic customer relationships, understand their needs and deal with any difficult situations as they arise.

1 **Reflecting.** Reflecting back the emotion(s) you are sensing from the customer, e.g. 'You seem to be very frustrated by that.' 'Would I be right in saying that this is very important

to you?' 'From what you're telling me it appears that you are happy to...'

2 **Summarising**. In précis (short), summarising an entire chunk of speech, e.g. in bullet-point form: 'So you bought the outfit on Wednesday, it doesn't fit and you would prefer a refund rather that an exchange?'

3 **Paraphrasing**. Quoting word-for-word what someone has told you. This can be key words, a phrase, and an occasional sentence. Do this regularly and briefly during an exchange: 'You're looking for a smart suit...' 'It's for a conference...' 'Something not too formal.'

With all of these techniques, when you have reflected back, summarised or paraphrased, wait for confirmation from the customer to ensure that you have understood them correctly.

4 **Linear probing** (Q-A-Q-A-Q-A). Linear probing is a simple and highly effective technique. It involves using the answer to the previous question as the parent of the next. It requires the use of open questions as opposed to closed:

Open prefixes	Closed prefixes
What	Are you
When	Can you
Who	Should you
Where	Did you
How	Will you
Why	Would you
Which	Have you
Tell me	Do you
Explain	Is it
Describe	Does it
For what reason(s)	Could it
In what way(s)	
Give me an example	
Expand on that	

Open questions allow the customer to give more detail, and they are a great way of encouraging them to tell us more about how they are thinking and feeling. Also, they built rapport keeping the connection strong.

Linear probing also involves choosing a specific path, which you stick to until you have reached the important detail; then you can follow another line of questioning. You have to be focused and engaged to do this so it's a great way to control the barriers to listening.

---

brilliant example

Linear probing

'Can I help you find what you are looking for?'

'Yes please, I want a suit for a wedding that is not too formal and quite light as it's a summer wedding.'

(Choose a linear path to follow from the three provided i.e. suit for a wedding, not too formal, lightweight for summer.)

'When you say not too formal, what sort of thing did you have in mind?'

'Maybe something in linen that's not very fitted but still smart and quite neutral in colour.'

(Simply use the answer to this previous question as the parent of the next:)

'When you say neutral colour what neutral colours do you like?'

'Beige would be nice.'

(Then you can start a new line of questioning.)

I use the following 'LISTEN' acronym in my training courses as a simple way to remember what is important; even if you focus on the main headings it can really make a difference. Listening is an active skill and it takes practice like any other. The good news is that the breakdown of our normal communication is: writing 9%, reading 16%, talking 30%, listening 45%, so we have more opportunity to practise!

brilliant tip

Look for opportunities to use the 'LISTEN' acronym not just with customers but with work colleagues, friends, family even if they are challenging. You will be amazed by the effect.

L LOOK INTERESTED

Face the speaker.

Maintain good eye contact.

Stay relaxed.

Lean forward.

Maintain an open posture.

I INQUIRE WITH QUESTIONS

Clarify the speaker's meaning.

Probe to receive all the facts.

Use the various questioning techniques.

S STAY ON TARGET

Remember your objective – stick to the point.

Listen for the complete message; don't prejudge.

Don't interrupt (unless the respondent is straying from the point).

Think ahead.

T TEST YOUR UNDERSTANDING

Check that you understand what is being said – 'So what you are saying is...? (Use your own words to précis the respondent's reply.)

E EVALUATE THE MESSAGE

Identify the speaker's purpose.

Analyse what is being said and how it is being said (body language, pace, tone and pitch).

N NEUTRALISE YOUR FEELINGS

Don't react adversely to what you hear.

Don't become heated or emotional.

Keep an open mind.

Be enthusiastic; show a genuine interest.

Maintain self-control.

IT'S YOUR EARS THAT HEAR BUT YOUR MIND THAT LISTENS.

brilliant dos and don'ts

Do

✔ Make a real commitment to listen.

✔ Use positive open body language whether on the phone or face to face.

✔ Maintain a relaxed eye contact.

✔ Ask relevant questions to interrupt appropriately and maintain control.

✔ Question for more detail.

✔ Test assumptions with clarifying questions.

✔ Avoid making judgements.

✔ Paraphrase and summarise.

Don't

✘ Fidget or move around too much.

✘ Interrupt inappropriately.

✘ Follow your own agenda but go with the flow of the speaker.

✘ Make assumptions.

Listen between the lines

Having good powers of observation is also very important for getting a clear message from the customer. This includes being aware of their body language, facial expressions and the tone and pitch of their voice. These can all give us vital clues as to how the customer is feeling. If you pick up on the clues, use your questioning and clarifying skills to check your assumptions and understanding.

brilliant tips

Listening on the phone

- Be aware of the customer's voice. Listen for the volume, tone and pitch as they are really good clues as to how they are feeling. If the pitch or tone goes up or down, it indicates a change in the customer you are listening to. If this goes up, it can indicate that they are excited or enthused by something; if it goes down, it can indicate that they are resigned or view something negatively. An increase of pace suggests excitement, and a slowing down a calmness.

- Make sure when you are on the phone that you are free of visual distractions. Be careful of technology – email would possibly be the biggest one if you are at your computer or your mobile phone! Other distractions include television, miscellaneous papers on your desk or anything else that can take away your focus. When you're having a conversation with someone on the phone, it's no different from speaking to them in person. They deserve your complete and undivided attention. If you have something else that may take away your focus, you are doing your customer a disservice. Simply move it out of sight.

- When talking to clients on the phone, have a note pad on your desk so you can write down their name and company name.

There is nothing more embarrassing than to suddenly forget who you're talking to.

● Don't forget that just because they can't see you doesn't mean they don't feel the thread of connection breaking; eye contact on the phone is just as important as face to face.

● Adopt positive body language because it has a real effect on your voice and breathing. Sit up in your chair; smile. It's a bit of a cliché, but it does come across. I often tell customer service people to stand up if they are taking a challenging phone call. It's amazing how much stronger your voice will be when you're standing up and/or maintaining good posture when you take a call. It is no surprise that when your voice is stronger, your confidence is stronger too.

Body talk

He that has eyes to see and ears to hear may convince himself that no mortal can keep a secret. If the lips are silent, he chatters with his fingertips; betrayal oozes out of every pore.

Sigmund Freud

Just as being observant of others' body language and vocal tone is important we also need to be very aware of the impact we are having on the customer in front of us or on the phone. Our body language and vocal tone contribute greatly to the message we are giving and greatly to the thread of connection we have with the customer. If you watch a television drama with the sound turned off, you will be able to judge the mood of the actors. Their body movements and facial expression will reveal whether they are sad, happy, angry, pleased, hostile or friendly.

Research has shown that in a presentation before a group of people, 55% of the impact is determined by body language, 38% by tone of voice, and only 7% by the content of your presentation.

our body language and vocal tone contribute greatly to the message we are giving

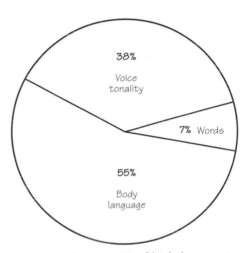

Figure 2.2 Comparison of the impact of body language, tone of voice and words
Source: Albert Mehrabian

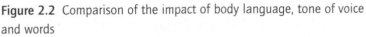

brilliant tips

Getting non-verbal communication right

● What is your body saying to the customer – are you slouched or leaning heavily on your desk or till? It sounds simple but it makes a huge difference to the impression you give if you keep your spine straight and your head up. Plant your feet firmly on the ground; this will also give you an air of confidence. It can be hard work to maintain positive posture all day, but it really ▶

is the only way that the customers will get the best impression from you. Good posture goes a long way.

- You need to keep eye contact with the customer you are assisting at all times or at least 80% of the time. Keeping eye contact tells the customer that you are listening and care about what they have to say. If you are helping more than one customer, it is a good idea to spread the eye contact around.

- Be aware of facial expressions and gestures. For example, raised eyebrows can make you look like you doubt what the customer is saying; blown out cheeks suggest exasperation. We naturally tend to move our hands about when we speak. Most of the time these movements don't mean very much but some gestures are full of meaning, like a clenched fist moved rapidly, pointing or hands thrown up in despair. Other parts of the body are used in gestures: shrugged shoulders, head thrown back, a foot stamped can show frustration or disapproval, none of which the customer wants to see.

- Watch your distance; stand too close and at best you are invading the customer's space and at worst it can come across as threatening and intimidating. Stand too far away and you will appear aloof.

- How are you standing/sitting? People co-operating tend to be at an angle of about 45 degrees to each other. People confronting each other, or in a superior/subordinate relationship, tend to be face to face. Turning away during communication gives a definite signal of hostility or disinterest.

- Are you giving out mixed messages? Because most of us are very good at reading body language instinctively, we need to be careful that our physical impact is complementing the message we want to give. For example, if we say to a customer that we understand their concern but our body is saying we really aren't interested, then the customer will see and feel this; this could escalate the situation or leave the customer feeling undervalued or angry.

● Tonal qualities make a difference to meaning. The most commonly used is the raised voice at the end of a statement that turns it into a question. 'It's time to go', means 'it's time to go'. 'It's time to go?' means 'is it time to go already?' We naturally pause to think and to listen. If we pause too long, it may show nervousness or boredom. If we pause too little, it may show nervousness again, or anger, or just being in a hurry. A raised voice can come across as angry, or keen to get a point across, or a need to dominate. If we talk very quietly, it can be interpreted as feeling unsure of ourselves or of what we are saying. Varying the tone of your voice can have a dramatic effect on the intimacy of the relationship. For example, if you ask, 'How do you feel?' in a very firm tone, the reply is likely to be superficial. If you ask the same question with a softer tone it is more likely to communicate empathy and concern.

The power of empathy

We will be looking at this in more detail in the chapter on dealing with customer complaints, but no chapter on the cornerstones of customer service would be complete without mentioning empathy.

brilliant definition

Empathy

This literally translates as *in feeling*; it is the capability to share another being's emotions and feelings. (Wikipedia)

To get empathy right we have to revisit our attitude towards the customer. We have to put ourselves in another's shoes. Imagine what it might be like to experience what they are feeling. We should do this because as customers ourselves we probably will have experienced at some time or other most of the same situations and emotions of our customers. On the other hand, if we don't value, respect and appreciate our customers, how can we possible feel empathy for them? Without this appreciation, empathy can come across as insincere and patronising. Empathy is essential because it's one of the best ways to defuse emotion, which is crucial when dealing with angry customers. Expressing empathy towards an upset customer absorbs the emotion, allowing the agitated customer space to think; this is because they are not being blocked by negative thoughts that come from feeling a situation is unfair, unjust or simply being misunderstood. If we simply and genuinely acknowledge the emotions, a customer can experience a positive effect; it's very important: only use empathy when you genuinely mean it.

brilliant tip

If you can't empathise with the customer at first, then adopt empathic listening, in other words, listen with understanding, suspending your own opinions and judgements and this will put you in the right place to find something you can genuinely empathise with.

What's in it for you as a service provider to empathise with a customer? Empathy can actually make the interaction with the emotional customer be resolved quicker, with improved results. Empathy allows you to connect with your customer, establish rapport and create a sense of teamwork between you. Once the customer realises that you are on their side, they become willing to work with you to fix the problem or allow you time to resolve the issue. This makes the resolution process pass quickly, because you are working together. The co-operation of the customer ensures that the resolution will be better.

 Two parts of empathy: skill (tip of iceberg) and attitude (mass of the iceberg).

Source unknown

There are ways to express your empathy, such as appreciative statements like: 'I can really see how this is frustrating for you'; 'I appreciate how you feel – I would feel the same in this situation'. But the most important thing is to adopt an empathic attitude throughout all your interactions with customers. Empathy and trust are a platform for effective understanding, communication and relationships. Empathy and trust are essential to develop solutions, win and retain business, and avoid or defuse conflict. Empathy and trust are essential for handling complaints and retaining customers.

▶ brilliant example

I work with a top cruise company and this example came from one of the team leaders in the service call centre. The customer missed a connection flight due to bad weather, causing them to miss the ship's sailing. Having booked a fly cruise, they were flown (by the cruise company) to Corfu to connect with the ship at its first port of call but luck had it that a bad storm prevented the ship from docking at Corfu making it impossible for them to join the ship. Since this was only a week-long cruise, they gave up and went home. This was a young couple with a five-year-old child, so naturally they were devastated and once back in the UK the wife rang the call centre in floods of tears. Although the fact that the cruise company was able to book them on another cruise for later in the year was welcomed, the customer remained really upset. Through empathic listening the team leader was able to identify the main reason for the upset. The ▶

lady had bought her son a tuxedo to wear on the formal night and had imagined the lovely photos of him dressed up. Now she feared he would have outgrown it by the time they took the cruise. Having children of her own, the team leader was genuinely empathic, understanding the woman's emotions exactly. This made the interaction a **wow** moment and the woman was left feeling the company not only behaved professionally, but they also cared about her family and her disappointment ... powerful stuff!

Personality counts

The case for understanding different types

It is no secret that, on the whole, we like people like ourselves; it feels more comfortable and easy if we 'click' with someone. We can be irritated by some people and we don't really know why; they just seem to grate on us, probably because they have different preferences, and as a result, can make us feel uncomfortable.

Recognising and reacting quickly to customers' personality types will help us to appreciate their differences and avoid being irritated, allowing us to adapt our behaviour so we are more 'acceptable' to them. If you have long-term customers that you have to account manage, then it's even more important you understand their type so you can develop the relationship.

Understanding your natural style

This is not about pigeon-holing you or the customer; it's about understanding and appreciating differences. Imagine that you have four barrels each containing a different behavioural style. You will have different levels of these behaviours in each of those barrels. Blended together this makes each of us a real mix of the four main personality styles. The fuller the barrel, the easier it is to flex that particular style. The emptier the barrel, the more difficult and uncomfortable it will feel. Also, it's only preferences that we are looking at; the model does not measure skills, intelligence, values or attitudes; they are simply behaviours. The important thing is to recognise which of your barrels are fuller (or emptier) and be aware of how it affects your interactions with customers.

Carl Gustav Jung, a leading light in twentieth-century psychology, was one of the first great thinkers to categorise people's 'personality types' according to simple, accessible criteria. He saw four main archetypes, displayed in Figure 2.3.

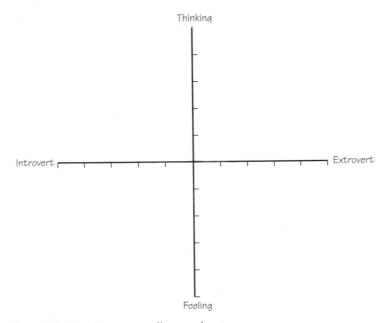

Figure 2.3 The four personality quadrants

The above figure indicates the two main factors:

1   How people tend to make decisions (represented by the vertical axis).

2   How people relate to others (represented by the horizontal axis).

From it we can see that people range from those who base decisions on pure logic/reason to those who predominantly take
action on feelings or 'gut instinct'. It also shows that people
range from those who seek to interact greatly with others, to
those who prefer not to dominate and vocalise to a greater
degree but to remain closed to their own inner experiences.

Jung termed the former type an 'extrovert' and the latter an
'introvert'. There is confusion about these terms. Some think
introverts are shy, lack confidence and extroverts are confident
and secure, but this is not necessarily true. Extroverts simply
'take energy from outside' and introverts 'take energy from
within', as shown in Figure 2.4.

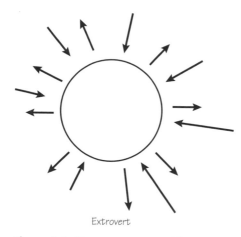
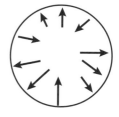

Extrovert   Introvert

Figure 2.4 How extroverts and introverts use energy differently

If you don't know what an extrovert is thinking, you
haven't listened; if you don't know what an introvert is
thinking, you haven't asked.

Source unknown

Before you apply this to other people, it is a good idea to have an understanding of your own preferences. Use the following four question sets (A, B, C and D) to help you identify whether your more comfortable behaviour is introvert or extrovert. If you think the statement refers to you, give it a cross, if not, leave it blank.

A questions

Do you:

- Hesitate giving an immediate response to a question, preferring to think through your response before answering no matter how quickly you do that?   _____

- Have difficulty in putting over your point of view and often find yourself becoming frustrated because someone else makes a point you have already thought about and you were not given the time and space to express it?   _____

- Become upset when you are interrupted whilst expressing views and opinions. You take the view that because you are polite in allowing people the opportunity to express their viewpoint you should receive the same courtesy.   _____

- Get bored with idle chatter and chit chat?   _____

- If you have a problem, prefer to think about it before telling other people?   _____

B questions

Do you:

- Speak first before thinking, where you are talking out your thoughts?   _____

- Become easily engaged in conversation, even with strangers, and then tend to dominate the conversations?   _____

- Perceive telephone calls, even in the midst of meetings and discussions, as a welcome interruption as opposed to a distraction? ____

- Feel more comfortable working and generating ideas with a group rather than working alone? ____

- When you have a problem, like to talk to other people about it and then think it through yourself? ____

Now place yourself (X) on the Introvert–Extrovert scale (Figure 2.5). *A questions* represent introverted behaviour and *B questions* represent extroverted behaviour. If you have equal scores, this does suggest that both of these barrels are close together which is absolutely fine; it means that you have adapted the behaviours really well so they are now very close. If this is the case, go with the side that you feel instinctively is where you are most comfortable.

Introvert ┌──┬──┬──┬──┬──■──┬──┬──┬──┐ Extrovert

Figure 2.5 The introvert–extrovert scale

If you think about how you connect with customers, whether they are introvert or extrovert can have a major impact on how they respond to you. It's still important to establish the connection with eye contact and a smile if face to face and your focus and verbal tone if on the phone, but if they respond in a very upfront way wanting to create more energy from the interaction they are probably displaying more extrovert behaviour. If they seem to be more hesitant or softer in their energy, they are more likely to be displaying introverted behaviour. To maintain the connection with extroverts, you need to build on the energy and with introverts you need to give them more space and time to react.

Now we are going to look at decision making and whether you prefer to use logic and facts or whether you go with your gut feelings.

C questions

Do you:

- Prefer to settle an argument based on facts rather than on what will keep the peace? _____

- Behave so strong-mindedly that if you disagree with someone you will tell them even though it may be kinder to say nothing and let them go on thinking they are right? _____

- Make important decisions easily and have difficulty understanding why people get uptight about matters that are not relevant to the matter in hand? _____

- Believe that it is not particularly necessary to like people – or be liked yourself – in order to be able to work with them? _____

- Feel sceptical about things until you have assimilated all the facts? _____

D questions

Do you:

- Make decisions based on other person's feelings? _____

- Sacrifice your own comfort in order to accommodate others? _____

- Question decisions that will affect the welfare of others? _____

- Immediately refute something you have said and which has given offence, thus causing people to perceive you as weak willed? _____

- Perceive harmony as preferable to 'being correct', thus avoiding conflict? _____

Now place yourself (X) on the thinking–feeling scale (Figure 2.6). *C questions* represent thinking behaviours and *D questions* represent feeling behaviours. Again, if you have equal scores, go with the side that you feel instinctively more comfortable with.

Thinking

Feeling

Figure 2.6 The thinking–feeling scale

How our customers make decisions couldn't be more important. We want them to make the vital decision to do business
with us again and again. If we can tap into their main preference, this will help us present our products and services to them
in a way that they can make the decision comfortably and, as
a result, feel better about their decision. A quick recap: for the
thinkers, facts, reason and logic will appeal to them; there is no
point in using emotion at the first stage of their decision making
as it will just annoy them. For the feelers, giving them logic
and facts will bore them and they will lose interest. The two
preferences, of course, interact with each other, for example,
an introverted thinker will be hard to draw out. Imagine if they
were not happy with your product or service, the chances are
they won't tell you. They will do lots of thinking and you may
get an email or a letter if you are lucky, but most likely they
will not say anything. Figure 2.7 is a model showing how the

preferences interact with each other. We will refer back to this model in other chapters of this book.

You can now plot both of your crosses on the axes in Figure 2.7. This will give you an idea of what behaviours are most natural to you. You will predominantly be in one coloured quadrant, and the closer you are to an axis, the more likely you are to have an ability to adapt into those behaviours.

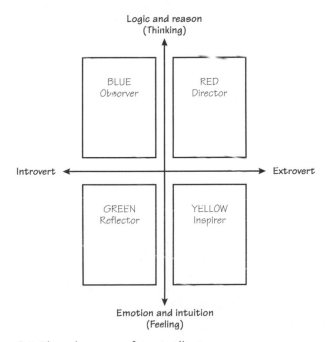

Figure 2.7 The colour axes of personality types

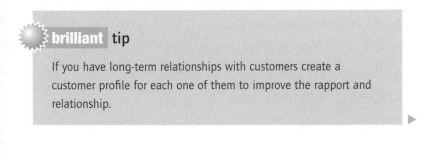

brilliant tip

If you have long-term relationships with customers create a customer profile for each one of them to improve the rapport and relationship.

1   Decide what their main behavioural style is, based on your observations so far and using the descriptions in this chapter.

2   Look at your current relationship: where it is strong and what are the challenges in the relationship?

3   Set a relationship strategy. For example, if your customer is an introverted thinker and you are an extrovert and you feel you have a tendency to interrupt them, give them enough space to talk. This could be a good objective to start with.

Characteristics of personality types

Driver: red (driven by the task and results)

- High energy
- Sharp and pointed body language
- Expressive
- Vocally they speak quickly and sharply
- Irritated by chit chat
- Easily irritated and quick to react
- Objective-focused
- Know what they want and how to get there!
- Communicates quickly, gets to the point
- Sometimes tactless and brusque
- Can be an 'ends justify the means' type of person
- Hardworking, high energy
- Does not shy away from conflict

Expressive: yellow (driven by being popular and liked)

- Quick to smile and engage
- More rounded and expressive with their gestures

- Open body language
- Like to talk a lot – everyone is a potential new friend
- Natural salespeople or story-tellers
- Warm and enthusiastic
- Good motivators, communicators
- Can be competitive
- Can tend to exaggerate, leave out facts and details
- Sometimes would rather talk about things than do them!

Amiable: green (driven by wanting to please)

- Have a need to connect and trust you
- Soft and rounded gestures
- A quiet and reflective energy
- Have a need to preserve their privacy
- Softly spoken, often leaving silences which they are comfortable with
- Kind-hearted people who avoid conflict
- Can blend well into any situation
- Can appear wishy-washy – has difficulty with firm decisions
- Highly sensitive and emotional

Analytical: blue (driven by getting things right)

- Can seem detached, cold and unemotional
- Closed or contained body language
- Tend to speak only when necessary
- Uncomfortable with chit chat
- Highly detail oriented people
- Can have a difficult time making decisions without ALL the facts
- Tend to be highly critical people

- Can tend to be pessimistic in nature
- Conservative and avoid taking risks
- Very perceptive

No one personality type outshines the other or is preferable to the other – but all complement each other in different ways. Especially in long-term relationships, if you can adapt your behaviour so your customer feels more comfortable dealing with you, you will build trust and respect and, as a result, maintain and get more business.

brilliant tips

The yellow

Brief and fleeting contact

- A warm and friendly interaction
- Chit chat
- A personal touch
- Use their name

Long-term relationship

- A friendly, informal and relaxed relationship
- Fun and personal
- High energy and spontaneous
- Not too much pressure

The blue

Brief and fleeting contact

- Respectful and polite
- Not too personal
- Time to think
- Slower pace and calmer energy

Long-term relationship

- Formal and professional
- Facts and figures, non-emotional
- Calm and composed
- To be listened to with space to speak

The green

Brief and fleeting contact

- Friendly but not personal
- Empathic and sensitive
- Gentle energy
- Genuine interest

Long-term relationship

- An unpressured, harmonious and friendly relationship
- Mutual trust
- Space to speak, respectful listening
- Loyalty and honesty

The red

Brief and fleeting contact

- High energy, efficient and quick
- No chit chat
- Respect for their status
- Direct and results oriented

Long-term relationship

- Efficient and results driven, built on respect
- Outcomes and benefits
- Task focused and quick
- Need to feel they are very important

Rate yourself to stay on track: the connection circle

Use this as a way to evaluate your ability to connect and interact positively with customers. This is a self-audit exercise in which you rate yourself according to how well you believe you do the following. Rate yourself on a scale of 1 to 5, where 5 is 'Excellent' and 1 is 'Extremely poor'. Plot the scores on the connection circle to identify your key priorities for developing the necessary skills. Use this circle regularly to check your progress. An example of a completed connection circle is illustrated by Figure 2.8.

Maintaining a positive and appreciative attitude towards
the customers   ___ /5

Establishing and maintaining the thread of connection   ___ /5

Listening properly to customers   ___ /5

Asking customers questions to understand them properly___ /5

Taking a genuine interest in customers   ___ /5

Showing genuine empathy   ___ /5

Maintaining positive body language/vocal tone   ___ /5

Recognising and adapting to different personality
preferences   ___ /5

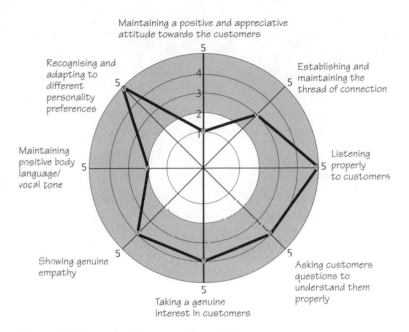

Figure 2.8 Example of a connection circle

Customer service managers

As a final note to this chapter, if you manage a customer service team, look to recruit staff that like people and appreciate customers. Train them in the soft skills that have been described. Although people skills are often seen as natural, they don't necessarily come naturally; they have to be worked at and focused on and never taken for granted. Use the connection circle to help your staff evaluate themselves and identify training needs.

brilliant recap

- Get your attitude right towards your customers; adopt a policy of respect and appreciation.

- Build and maintain the thin thread of connection, through focused listening and positive body language, whether you are working face to face or on the phone.

- Adopt an empathic attitude and always be genuine.

- Understand your own personality preferences and be flexible with your customers making yourself easy to do business with.

- Use the connection circle to measure your performance.

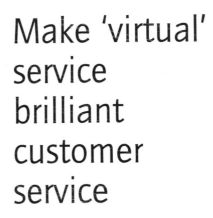

CHAPTER 3

Make 'virtual' service brilliant customer service

*If you make customers unhappy in the physical world, they might
each tell six friends. If you make customers unhappy on the Internet,
they can each tell 6,000 friends.*

Jeff Bezos (founder of Amazon)

I am no expert in technology and, in fact, my husband laughs
at me for my lack of knowledge. I also seem to have a strange
effect on it where it often goes wrong for me and then works
perfectly well for someone else. What I am is totally addicted to
is buying products and services over the Internet, and I know
what works for me and what doesn't. It's really important to
recognise that customers always want the same things no matter
how they go about getting them. The Internet has made customer service easier in some ways and more difficult in others.
This chapter looks at key priorities when providing service on
the Internet. As with all customer service, most of it is obvious
but it doesn't mean that we always do it.

The fantastic Internet

The Internet has changed the way we do just about everything.
I don't know what I would have done without it writing this
book; it makes things so much easier and so much quicker and
has opened us all up to 24-hour business. You can now book
a holiday at three o'clock in the morning or order a CD you

the Internet can provide the most stress-free shopping ever

have just seen advertised on the TV at 10 o'clock at night. Everything is possible. We don't have to travel or get addresses; it can provide the most stress-free shopping ever and we have access to millions of products and services from all over the world. What does this mean to customer service though? It should mean that we have many more opportunities than ever to offer brilliant service, for example:

- useful websites that offer information to the customers whenever they need it giving them total independence;
- interactive programs that give the customers a pre-experience before they buy;
- tracking systems to allow customers to be more in control;
- follow-up emails to encourage feedback after a purchase;
- the opportunity to inform customers of special offers and new products.

All of these services are great when they work well. The challenge is they can be as equally off-putting if they are done wrong. As with all forms of business, providing good customer service is a must for Internet marketers. There is no reason why an Internet-based business should provide any different standard of customer service than other businesses. In fact, having an Internet-based business is a big reason to step up your customer service efforts. Why? Because the competition is enormous. You are not just competing in a high street; you are competing in a worldwide market and it is no effort for a customer to close down your site and go on to another. Also, just because they have bought from you before does not mean you can take it for granted that they will do so again; you have to work even harder at building customer loyalty. So don't forget they are already on the Internet when doing business and so will have no problem sharing their bad experiences with the whole Internet community!

> it is no effort for a customer to close down your site and go to another

Benefits for doing business online

Let's just remind ourselves of the reasons for offering our customers the opportunity to do business on the Internet:

- You are offering customers an opportunity to buy from you at any time 24 hours a day.

- They can find out about products in advance in their own way and their own time and then still come and buy from you direct more informed. The Internet enables you to showcase your products, provide up-to-date information, specifications and applications, as well as sell products all in one place. The information provided on the Internet, as well as product offerings, can be changed or updated instantly.

- The Internet allows you to communicate with your customers on an individual basis easily and inexpensively.

- You are able to promote your products to a much larger audience than may otherwise have come into contact with your business thus allowing you to promote yourself as a global company.

- It can save you and the customer time and money. The web eliminates many of the extra costs that are associated with ordering, travelling for example. This allows you to give customers better value for money and to be more competitive.

- A major benefit of ordering from the web is that it allows for efficient tracking of orders. Once logged on, customers are able to look up their order history to quickly see what they have ordered in the past.

● You can track your customers and understand more about
their buying patterns, enabling you to tailor your marketing
accordingly.

What do customers want?

What the stats say

● Between 50 and 75% of consumers do not complete online
purchases of items they want because of poorly designed
websites.

● The most frequent button clicked on e-retail sites is the
'back' button, which is an indication of people's frustration
with poor website design.

● The top customer complaints about online shopping
according to customer surveys are:

  ● slow websites – 48%;

  ● products unavailable – 31%;

  ● late deliveries – 30%;

  ● inability to track orders – 25%;

  ● website outage – 22%.

The basic needs

These are the same universal needs that all customers have; let's
take a look at how they relate to the Internet.

● **Knowledge and information.** When we buy something
we want to know something about it: it could be the
benefits and how it will help us; it could be detailed
information about what the product or service will do for
us; it could be prices and guarantees. The difference on the
web is that the customer is in control so it's got to be easy
to find and quick. Customers don't have to be sensitive to
anybody's feelings if they don't get the information they
want quickly. They will just switch to another website.

- **Easy.** We hate it when we are given the run around by a call centre; we expect to be put through to the right person as quickly as possible without being passed round. On the web we have even less patience. I hate it if I have to go through too much procedure on a website. The thing is, I am shopping on the web to save time. If I wanted a lengthy experience, I would go the traditional route. So don't expect customers to give you lots of information before they get fed up.

- **Treated well.** Just because this is a website don't think you can get away with giving a customer an impersonal service; the basics like 'please' and 'thank you', etc. are still essential. Emails sent to confirm orders or inform customers of late delivery, etc. still have to treat the customer as a human being. When responding to a customer's questions by email it is so important to 'listen' to the customer and respond to ALL of their questions or issues (see Chapter 6 on handling all complaints).

- **Peace of mind.** One of the biggest worries for a customer purchasing online is trust, and how much of a risk it is buying online. Customers need to feel totally secure in the order and have the peace of mind to know they will get their money back or a replacement if something goes wrong. I find the star rating that eBay does for instance a real help when making buying decisions.

- **Getting what they want quickly.** I hate waiting very long for anything but when I order on the Internet I want it even quicker. The medium itself is so immediate that, again, customers are not very patient; they might buy from you once but you will lose customer loyalty if you don't get the products or services to them very quickly.

- **Help with problems.** Because we don't have to actually deal with anyone if we have problems, we are more likely to complain, because there is less of an emotional response.

This is good news for businesses but not if they ignore the complaint – because it is also easier to ignore, there is no emotional connection. Knowing that they can always contact a real person if all else fails is a real bonus for customers.

🔆 ▶**brilliant** example

Amazon is one of my favourite companies to do business with. I should have shares in it, given the amount of money I spend. It is a fantastic example of how virtual service can be brilliant, and this is why:

- The website is very quick and really easy to navigate. I love the feature where they can tell you what else you might be interested in. It is also really easy to search on the site.

- Information is easy to get if you want it but you are left in control.

- When you buy, because you sign in they remember your details so you don't have to put your address and credit card details in every time. I love this as so many other companies make you do it every time.

- There are several choices of delivery option for impatient people like me and most of them are free.

- The follow-up email confirming your order comes straight away and it's polite and human.

- It's easy to track your orders.

- The returns policy is straightforward and easy.

All this is great and keeps me coming back for more. And recently they went that bit further when I purchased a computer game in advance of the release date. When it came out it was cheaper to buy in the supermarkets so they informed me and refunded my credit card with the difference – brilliant stuff and absolutely no contact with a human being.

So we need to look at any Internet marketing of our business through our customers' eyes and bear the key needs above in mind. Even large companies get it wrong. I used a supermarket website to order all my Christmas shopping last year and it took me one very focused and careful hour to create a shopping basket that would be right for the special day. At the check out for some reason it would not take our address; it timed out and I lost the lot, including the delivery slot. When I rang the help line they were totally disinterested and told me I would have to do it again. Not only had I wasted an hour in front of the computer, I was now too late for any other delivery and so had to face the crowds at the supermarket. Even though this was my normal supermarket, I didn't go there and went to another one instead at which I am now a loyal customer. The website fiasco put me off a company that I had been shopping at for over 10 years. If you are going to go the virtual way, consider the basics below so you build customer loyalty rather than lose it.

Internet basics

- Build your site and services with your customer in mind. Develop an 'attitude' of good customer service by creating a site that is customer-friendly focused. To do this, be clear about what you're offering and what your site is about. Great content doesn't mean much if your visitors can't find it, so work to organise your site with titles and headings that are clear and descriptive with information that is logically organised and structured. If you have a call to action, such as a newsletter sign-up or special contest, don't be afraid to instruct your visitor to participate. Make it as easy as possible for your customer to search and use your site, and consider how long it takes to do anything that is requested of them, i.e. joining and signing up.

- Make sure that your company website communicates the passion for service that exists in the organisation. Websites are increasingly becoming the front door for businesses. A website is an extension of the company to prospects and customers in the same way that the receptionist or telephone operator is the front door to your company, and remember that customers make their judgement within tenths of a second.

brilliant tips

- Have a look at other companies' websites but visit them as a customer and note down what you like and dislike.
- Ask your customers what they want from your site.

- Keep the ordering process simple and straightforward. Consider all possibilities of questions, problems and issues that a customer might encounter. Eliminate all possibilities of confusion. One of the things that frustrates me is going through a whole process only to find at the final point I have to ring the company to order; it feels like I have been cheated and I often switch to another site.

- Immediately following an order, your customer should receive a confirmation email thanking them for their order. When the order has been shipped, your customer should receive a second email stating that the product has been despatched. Make sure these emails contain the human basics as these emails are the only way you have a chance to build rapport with you customers.

- Surprise your customers by exceeding their expectations. If your policy states that orders are received within 5–7 business days, try to achieve deliveries in 3–4 business days. It's always great to receive something sooner than you had anticipated, not to mention that your reputation will have just jumped tenfold.

- Have an order tracking facility; a lot of the enquiries that you'll receive from customers will be about the status of their orders. Automating the order-tracking process can free up time to manage the more pressing aspects of your business.

● State your guarantees, shipping and refund policies clearly. If you work in a retail business, make it easy for your customers to return items. Simple things like including return labels within the packaging helps tremendously. Provide shipping/delivery costs prior to checkout instead of surprising them with shipping costs upon payment. This will go a long way towards establishing customer loyalty. Remember that on the whole most people are fearful of buying over the Internet unless the company has an established reputation. If they have a good experience of buying from you they will keep coming back and because they feel safe they will also recommend you to others.

● Always provide addresses and working phone numbers of your business on every page of your site. The worst thing a customer can experience is to place an order online, have a problem, then call a phone number and receive no response or call back. This will lose you any trust you might have built up so far and lose you a customer.

---

brilliant example

I wanted to set up a regular order of organic vegetables to my door so I searched the net and found a great website which was clear and easy to order from. I was a little nervous because it was a farm and seemed a fairly small outlet, but I had seen its vans about so I went ahead with the order. I got a lovely email back welcoming me as a new customer and then looked forward to receiving my goods. For the next three weeks I got a lovely fresh box of fruit and vegetables every week to my door. One Friday the box didn't arrive and, as we were having guests for the weekend, I was disappointed. I rang the company from its contacts on the web and on   ▶

Saturday morning I got my normal box and an extra box of goodies that I hadn't ordered as compensation. I was delighted and because I really liked these extra items I started adding them to my regular order after that. I now really trust this company and would not use any other; it's easy and safe and I feel valued as a customer.

● If it is possible, have a live help desk with real people to help when things go wrong. The ability to have a conversation with a live representative goes a long way to make the shopping experience more satisfying and help the customer feel more secure. If you do have this facility, advertise it on your site stating the times clearly when a customer can contact you. It is a real selling point.

brilliant tip

Live chat is another good option for most start-up e-businesses. It gives you the option of providing real-time help to more than one customer at a time. The downside is that you or your employees have to staff the chat utility. Make sure that your site clearly states when representatives are available to help. Once you have set your live chat hours, do your best to stick to them.

Using a live chat utility is much like instant messaging. After you install the utility on your site, customers can simply click on a link to contact you immediately. Normally, a small browser window will open, and you can communicate with your customer in real time.

● Respond to all email and phone enquiries within 48 hours, or sooner if you possibly can, otherwise they will go to the competition. And when we talk about responding, make it a personalised response that comes straight from you. Don't have an auto responder as your only form of communication.

- If you address all questions, enquiries and complaints promptly and in a personal manner, people will notice that you really care about their concerns; at your actual, real outlet, you wouldn't leave your customers standing there while you were busy with something else. No offline business could get away with this for long!

- Check on your customers after placing an order. Thank them a second time for ordering. Solicit your services should they have questions or problems. Also keep your customers aware of new offerings via email (but only with their permission). You'll give them additional value without their having to return to your site. Amazon does this with me and I love it.

- Provide a FAQs section on your website. Did you know that more than 80% of all customer questions are usually answered by just 20% of a support knowledge base? A page of frequently asked questions on your website will answer their questions before they ask them, by allowing your customers to be in control. I hate it if I am searching on the web and have to call a company to get a question answered – I feel the information should be on the site.

- Let your customers rate you and your site. Ask your customers to complete a simple customer service survey. Keep the survey quick and simple and allow for comments. Take careful note of what your customers say and work to make improvements accordingly.

brilliant tip

Offer the customer something for giving you feedback, such as a free gift discount off products or give them free entry into a competition. Be prepared for an overwhelming response because the great thing about the Internet is that people are more likely to give feedback as it seems less personal.

The basic ideas above are fundamental to delivering brilliant virtual service. However, you can't expect to run a business and remain completely anonymous – you have to give people some personal connection. Chapter 2 on the cornerstones of brilliant customer service is just as relevant on the Internet as it is face to face and on the phone. If you can find a way to really give brilliant personal service on the web, it will put you ahead of the game because only a very few companies get it completely right.

brilliant recap

- The Internet is a fantastic opportunity to expand your business and improve your service to your customers.

- Be aware of the main customer complaints when using the web, slow websites being the worst.

- No matter how customers buy services and products, they still want the same basic things. It is delivered differently via the Internet but it is still all about the personal experience.

- Understand the customer's basic needs and be sure to deliver them the way that is best for them. Gather feedback from your customers to make sure this happens.

- Look to companies that have already succeeded in delivering virtual service brilliantly. Study them and learn from them. If you can offer a personal service via the web, it will put you ahead of the competition.

CHAPTER 4

Use the 'emotional scale' to create loyalty and trust

The emotional experience

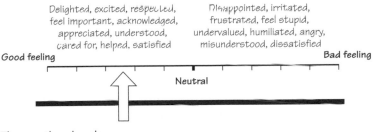

Delighted, excited, respected,
feel important, acknowledged,
appreciated, understood,
cared for, helped, satisfied

Disappointed, irritated,
frustrated, feel stupid,
undervalued, humiliated, angry,
misunderstood, dissatisfied

Good feeling

Bad feeling

Neutral

The emotional scale

After seeing my daughter off on a gap year and feeling totally grief stricken, I decided to book a cheap and cheerful holiday to Majorca for a week with my husband and son using a well-known, low-cost airline. We arrived at the airport expecting to be treated like sheep and ready to endure a couple of hours of torture in order to get away. I wasn't disappointed. Our first experience at the check-in desk was after at least 30 minutes of queuing even though we had supposedly checked in online. Our bags were overweight and we would have to make them lighter or pay an extortionate excess baggage charge. Admittedly, we had not read all the information on the website and made a mistake, but the website was particularly unclear, and judging by the number of other people in the same position, it wasn't just us that had got it wrong. There was almost an attitude of glee from the person at check-in, telling us the bad news, and then she could not have been more disinterested when it came to helping us with options on how to solve our problem: 'There are weighing scales over there' (pointing without looking at us) 'Come back to the queue when you are ready.'

Wheeling our luggage in the general direction of where she had waved, we could not find the scales. Eventually, after asking at another check-in desk of the same airline, and made to feel completely stupid, we were given clearer directions. Placing 50p in the slot, the weight of the suitcase was registered, and then the machine froze; to re-check the weight you had to pay another 50p and so on until you were certain. This had to be repeated with all three cases, costing around £10. You can imagine the fuss to get change: 10 minutes getting £10 worth of 50 pence pieces. It was a totally degrading (all of our personal items all over the airport floor) and frustrating experience. The airline charged over £10, which is obviously the intention, but now it had three very irritated customers, not to mention the queue of other customers waiting to use the same scales!

We then went back to the queue, which thankfully was now only two deep, to check in our bags. This time they all went through OK, although the engagement from the check-in staff was minimal. Just when we thought we could go through and get a large glass of something cold and alcoholic to calm us down and put us in a holiday mood, we were told to put our hand luggage in the basket to check that it was the right size. It is worth mentioning that I have travelled all over the world with this piece of hand luggage and it has never been refused by any airline. However, because I had filled it with stuff from my case to get the weight down, it was as fat as it has ever been and it wouldn't go in completely. Without looking up the assistant said, 'It's too large, you will have to go and buy another one that's smaller and you need to hurry up; check in closes in 10 minutes.' I stupidly started to explain that it was just a little fatter than usual because of the other suitcases but she just kept saying 'Sorry madam, it has to fit in completely. I can check it in but it will cost...' At that point, my son opened the bag, took out two jumpers, put them on over his clothes, shut the case and then forced it into the basket.

It was all so unnecessary; as soon as we walked away we put the jumpers back in the bag. I see this airline putting revenue generation way above the customers' needs and emotions, which leaves you feeling ripped off and unappreciated. To top off this experience, when getting on the plane we were greeted by a smiling steward saying 'Have a nice flight and enjoy your experience.' At this point nothing could have put us back up the emotional scale anywhere close to 'enjoying' our experience. We vowed that, unless there was no other choice, we would never travel with this airline again. (As I travel at least 20 times a year all over the world and the UK, this could have been a lot of business.) The knock-on effect is, as you can imagine, the large number of people we told about our experience, advising them to avoid the same experience.

A recent survey by Lee Resources Inc. found that it takes 12 positive service incidents to make up for one negative incident. We have so much choice today. We are rapidly moving from a service economy to an experience economy. As a result, as customers we don't just want services and products of high quality we also want positive, emotionally sensitive and memorable experiences. If you are able to understand the customers' emotional scale, you can get ahead of your competition and build trust and loyalty. You will also get recommended; nothing stays with us longer than a great feeling we have had from a great service experience and it gives us confidence to recommend a company to others.

> we are rapidly moving from a service economy to an experience economy

Moments of truth

So what is the emotional scale? It is a series of emotions customers go through during any interaction with a business. These
emotions usually result from one or more 'moments of truth'. As
customers ourselves we will have several 'moments of truth' in
any interaction with a business.

brilliant definition

Moments of truth

In 1986 Jan Carlzon, the former president of Scandinavian Airlines,
wrote a book entitled *Moments of Truth*.

In the book, Carlzon defines the moment of truth in business as:

> *Any time a customer comes into contact with any aspect of
> a business, however remote, is an opportunity to form an
> impression.*

He used the term to mean those moments in which important
brand impressions are formed and where there is significant
opportunity for customers to experience good or bad emotions.

Moments of truth can be first impressions or when customers have
certain expectations and they are disappointed, then they can form
very negative impressions or feel let down, undervalued or ripped
off.

From this simple concept, Jan Carlzon took an airline that was
failing and turned it round to be one of the most respected airlines
in the industry.

If we use my experience with a low-cost airline as an example,
we can start to see the main 'moments of truth':

● **The website**. We had to check in online on the company's
website. I found it frustrating, confusing, and full of extra

charges; definitely a negative moment of truth leading to feelings of being deliberately ripped off, and added to this I was irritated by the amount of time it took.

- **The check-in queue.** There were not enough staff and even after checking in online, the queue was still very long, taking 30 minutes; another negative moment of truth leading to the emotions of feeling undervalued and treated like sheep.

- **Check-in desk.** Rude and officious staff more concerned with terms and conditions and money making than the customer's needs. Again, the moment of truth was negative and the emotion was feeling stupid and humiliated.

- **Weighing scales.** Not just having to pay, but having to pay every time we needed to re-weigh the cases! Another negative moment of truth and definitely feeling that we were not valued and just there to make them as much money as possible regardless of how it made us feel.

- **Second check-in desk.** Another dismissive and rude check-in person who insisted that our hand luggage was too large, despite explanations. Yet another negative moment of truth with the emotion of anger and a feeling of never using this airline again if we can help it.

- **On boarding the plane.** A pleasant smile, warm eye contact and positive body language: this and a genuine greeting was a positive moment of truth, however, because of previous negative moments and where we registered on the emotional scale, it did nothing to change our mind. It was too little too late!

These are several main moments of truth, and while they may be the most important, there were lots of smaller ones as well. For example, you might find yourself walking towards your gate and encounter a couple of airline employees. They look up and smile at you. Now you may think that to be a small moment of truth, but it is an important one. It adds to the customer's total experience. Moments of truth are experienced by the customer as *bad, neutral* or *wow*, and the more wow moments they have, the more likely they are to go away with a good feeling about you or your business.

brilliant definitions

Bad

A moment where a customer has a negative experience which brings about damaging emotions.

Neutral

A moment where a customer's expectations are met but nothing more, which does not create any real emotion either way. Too many of these and they create an overall feeling of dissatisfaction.

Wow

A moment where a customer is surprised by how good something or someone is, where their expectations have been surpassed, leaving them with a good feeling about the business.

brilliant example

I had a really good example of one such 'wow' moment at a local Las Iguanas restaurant. We eat at this restaurant a lot as it is a favourite with my teenage children and it is getting a couple of mentions in this book because its approach to service is brilliant. On this occasion we were there having some cocktails, Friday night happy hour two for one. Deputy Manager, Alejandra Friess recognised us and came over to say hello, as usual remembering all our names. She asked us if we were eating and we told her we were cutting back and trying to save money for a holiday but we were enjoying the cocktails. Ten minutes later she appeared with a plate of nachos with all the trimmings which she knows is a family favourite. 'On the house for the nice family', she said. We were wowed because it was so unexpected and we were really hungry! There is so much choice of restaurants in our town and they are opening up all the time but we keep going back to this one. Yes, the food is good but most importantly we always feel good when we go there and it's a happy family experience.

Wow moments don't always have to cost you or the company you work for money. Remembering a customer's name or some personal details about them, their favourite drink, or table or the type of products they normally buy, or sometimes just stopping and interacting with a customer is enough. Any company and every customer service representative can create wow moments.

> wow moments don't always have to cost you or the company money

brilliant tips

Take a look at your business or the part of the business you are responsible for. What are the moments of truth for your customers (looked at the through the customers' eyes rather than your own filter)? Identify the main ones and consider how you can turn these into wow moments. If it's not your business, take responsibility for your moments of truth like our waitress; it could make all the difference on the emotional scale and it's fun! It may be a very small difference, but to the customer it changes a neutral moment into a wow moment.

If you manage people who interact with customers, make them all aware of the moments of truth. Some people think customer satisfaction isn't their responsibility but if they have an interface

▶

with a customer at any point, they could be responsible for a moment of truth.

Take a look at every point of contact from the website, the initial contact on the phone or face to face to how the interaction is completed. The end of the journey is just as important as the beginning because human nature dictates that we always remember the last negative experience more than all the positive ones that come before it.

Make the most of all your moments of truth. Welcome every one, even if they are negative moments such as complaints; see them as opportunities to show how good you and your organisation are. It will go a long way in building long-term customer loyalty and total customer satisfaction.

The good-feeling/bad-feeling business

In the world of customer service there is one reality you can't escape. Service is an emotional experience, not a series of facts and figures. Service is not a logical experience but an emotional one. You want to understand the ramifications of each emotion and how each impacts the moments of truth with your customers.

service is an emotional experience, not a series of facts and figures

So many businesses try to apply logic to customer service. They love to publish statistics on how satisfied their customers are. I was in a tyre workshop recently, a difficult experience most of the time. It's almost as if they have thought, 'This is a really unpleasant place to spend time waiting so let's just make it even worse, turn down the heating, decorate the walls with inappropriate posters and add a nasty, damp smell.' Strangely, this garage was also decorated with customer service slogans. One sign bragged of a 96% customer approval rating. When I asked the manager what that meant, he told me that only 4% of the customers complained. We will talk about how silence isn't a good sign later on in the book but never rate your customer service and moments of truth by how many complaints you get!

It's much harder to provide a great customer service than I would have ever realised. It's much more art than science in some of these other areas and not just about the facts but about how you are conveying them.

David Yu, Chief Operating Officer, Betfair

Delivering quality service that meets or exceeds your customer's expectations is more challenging than ever before. All businesses are different and I have worked in many large companies, some that sell products in the retail market and others are more business to business. From a customer service perspective, I believe that there are two kinds of service businesses. The first is the service or product where, even before the customer has any interaction with the company, the customer has a good feeling, helping to push them up the emotional scale. For example, if you are about to go to a luxury spa, you will already be in a 'good-feeling place'. On the other hand, the second type of business puts you in a 'bad-feeling place' at the other end of the emotional scale, before you even start. For instance, the tyre shop or the dentist! In a good-feeling business, customers are generally excited to book that holiday, buy the silk outfit, purchase their new sports car or look forward to a special dinner. It's much harder to give a customer a negative emotional experience if you work in a good-feeling business. You would have to answer your mobile phone while they were waiting to be served, answer the phone like you don't care, put customers on hold without telling them. When they come in you need to avoid looking at them and act as if they don't exist, avoid smiling. If they complain, give them no empathy and make them feel they are to blame; you must act like you don't care. This might sound silly but this is exactly what some businesses do: they take a good-feeling business and make the customer feel bad. If you are lucky enough to work in a good-feeling business, build on this positive emotion and work your customer up the scale.

In a bad-feeling business, delivering quality service is more challenging. Someone breaks your windshield, you have a flat tyre or you have the tooth ache from hell. You're hardly going to be in a positive emotional place. Although meeting service expectations is always difficult, it becomes more so in bad-feeling businesses. Customers are unhappy before they make contact. It's hard to imagine anybody getting excited because they have to get new tyres and then like me, they end up in their local tyre shop, sitting in that dirty, cluttered waiting area listening to the shrieking air tools. If they are lucky, they'll be offered a cup of salty liquid from a machine thinly disguised as coffee, and they will need it to help keep warm in the freezing, damp room.

What sort of business are you in? A good-feeling business or bad-feeling one? You may not have thought of it this way before but it's important because you either build on excellent emotions and energy or snuff it out with a poor first impression, alternatively focusing on moving customers from their bad-feeling place back up the scale. In either type of business, customer service is an emotional reaction.

You can't express emotions as numbers because they are harder to manipulate and considerably more difficult to manage. Imagine telling someone how much you love them by scoring them out of 10. You could try it, but I bet you get an extreme emotional response! Emotions are unpredictable, spontaneous and they happen in the now! Your ability to prepare for and manage these emotions will ultimately define your service success.

What creates bad moments of truth?

- **An unwelcoming environment**. This can be the actual environment the customer experiences, such as a waiting room, reception area, shop or restaurant, or it could be your website or call-centre management system. If it's a physical environment, it's not just what the customer sees; it can be what they smell, hear and how they feel. Is your business environment welcoming, comfortable and enjoyable for the customer to be in? Is it appropriate to your business? For example, walking into a trendy shop with loud music and staff with coloured hair and body piercings is fine for that type of business, but imagine the same scenario in a dentist's waiting room! If the environment is a virtual one, is it quick and efficient and easy to understand? Would it irritate you if you were the customer?

- **Ignoring the customer**. Speaking to colleagues, looking at a mobile phone, computer or answering the phone. It's so strange to me that you can be with someone in a shop or hotel and you are in the middle of a transaction of some sort and the phone rings and they answer it rather than continuing, if the ringing phone is annoying ask the customer if they would prefer you to answer it but don't make them feel totally unimportant by taking the call ahead of them.

- **Unwelcoming staff**. It's true what they say about never having a second chance to make a first impression. Use everything we looked at in Chapter 2 on the cornerstones of customer service to make a strong thread of connection and then work hard to maintain it.

- **Rudeness**. It's obvious but if you are looking through the wrong coloured filter for whatever reason, and we all have bad days, this will finish any chance of the customer leaving you at the good-feeling end of the emotional scale!
- **Inflexible, rigid bureaucracy**. Think about how you feel when someone quotes terms and conditions at you as an excuse for not being able to help. Are your terms and conditions and systems there to help the customer or control them? Be as flexible as you can and always make an effort to help the customer. Avoid saying things like: 'It is company policy'; 'I am not authorised to do that'; 'There is nothing I can do'; 'You should have noted the person's name'; 'We have no choice but to...'
- **Making excuses and not taking responsibility**. This one can be particularly irritating, especially when talking to a call centre and you keep being passed round with no one taking responsibility. Do whatever you can to help the customer. I was doing some coaching in a call centre recently and a customer service operator took a call from one such customer who was enquiring about times of flights for their cruise. The customer service operator responsible for booking cruises could not access details for the flights. As the customer was already upset and irritated, having been passed round several different sections, he took responsibility and rang the flight desk whilst the customer was on hold. He managed to get the information and relayed it back to the customer. The customer was so relieved and grateful; the bad moment had been turned round into a wow moment because this agent made a real commitment to helping the customer. Don't be in denial, take responsibility!
- **Blaming the customer when things go wrong**. This is another example of not taking responsibility. Always apologise, even if it's for how the customer is feeling and then seek to understand their problem.

- **Not keeping a promise**. If you promise the customer something, you have to deliver, otherwise don't promise it in the first place. If you promise them a call back at a particular time, then stick to it, even if you have nothing to tell them. It's fantastic to raise customers' expectations, but not if you can't meet them – this would be taking a wow moment and turning it into a bad one.

- **Ignoring a customer's needs**. I was recently on yet another plane and it was absolutely freezing because the air-conditioning was set too cold. There were no blankets provided and, in the end, I called a flight attendant and explained how cold I was. The response was unbelievable: 'Yes I know it's cold, other passengers have mentioned it, but as we have a full flight and we are having to work really hard to get everyone served, my staff need it cold at the moment. Have you a coat in the overhead locker you can get out to keep you warm?' Although I did have some sympathy for them, I was the one paying to sit in a freezer!

- **Not communicating**. When listening to various stories from people who travelled over Christmas 2009 with all the snow and bad weather, the biggest complaint was not the delays, the waiting, the lost of luggage or even totally ruined holidays; no, it was about the lack of communication and not being kept honestly informed. Even if the news is bad, it is better to inform the customer straight away and be honest about the situation.

---

brilliant example

Disney has a policy of asking front-line staff (cast members) to acknowledge a customer (guest) within 10 feet with a smile or a facial expression. Even describing customers as guests suggests that they see them through a positive filter. Below is the explanation as to why Disney has this policy.

▶

The front line is the bottom line

The employees in front of the customer are the ones they see – look after them, teach them well, support them. Every face to face interaction is a moment of truth. If a customer interacts with 60 cast members per day, there are 60 moments of truth. If there are 59 great moments and 1 bad, which do you think the customer will remember? We need all moments of truth to be great. They are how your company will be judged.

Disney customer service policy

A note to customer service managers

Whether you are big or small, you cannot give good customer service if your employees don't feel good about coming to work.

Martin Oliver, MD, Kwik-Fit Financial Services

If you manage customer service people, you need to be aware that they too register on an emotional scale. For whatever reason, if they are in the lower (feel bad) end of the scale, they are more likely to be looking at the customers through the grey negative filter. The front-line, customer service people are so vital to the customers' moments of truth, whether you are a good-feeling business or a bad-feeling business. Take time to motivate them up the emotional scale and you will see the bottom-line results.

brilliant tips

Motivating the customer service team

- Ironically, the first person who must be motivated is the manager. If you lack motivation or seem to be looking at customers through the wrong colour filter, you will lose any respect for your customer service initiative. You need to adopt a real passion and belief for your customer service policies and values; you also need to live them, leading from the front on everything. If you are excited and inspired to deliver wow moments of truth, your staff will be too. Make sure your enthusiasm is genuine; staff will sniff out any sign of a phoney rah-rah attitude.

- Hire motivated professionals. It's easier to hire motivated professionals than it is to motivate professionals. In your recruitment don't just interview for skills and experience, interview for attitude to people and customers. What colour filter are they already looking through? Remember, if you have a reputation for brilliance in service, you will attract people into your business wanting to be part of that good feeling. Disney is passionate about cleanliness. It hires only street sweepers and house cleaners who delight in cleaning. Result: Disney parks and resorts are immaculate.

- Measure and reward. Are you keeping score? Think about the tennis analogy. When you are warming up, hitting the ball to each other, how soon do you become bored and disinterested, wanting to play competitively? Is your team simply knocking balls to each other, or are they motivated by the competition between each other or with themselves to deliver brilliance? Find a way to measure something and then reward your team for their achievements. Make sure it's important, relevant to your team and it affects your bottom line; you will see everyone have a renewed energy.

▶

● Involve and listen to your team. They are on the front line; there is no one better in your business to give you feedback on customers' feelings and needs. I get paid to go into customer service departments and make recommendations on how to create the wow customer experience and the first thing I do is listen to members of the customer service team. It's so obvious and almost never done. Not only will the information and ideas be priceless, it will also create the feeling of inclusion and motivation will be high.

● Appreciate them and celebrate their successes. Look for opportunities to give genuine recognition for good work and celebrate success. It will breed more good work and more successes.

● Support and develop the team. Encourage them to handle more tricky situations, such as difficult interactions with customers and complaints. Coach them through these so they learn from the experience. Sometimes customer service can be a draining profession.

Companies that include their staff in the development and success of their customer service strategy are always more successful and success is more sustainable. Good feeling becomes part of the company culture and customers and staff can feel it when coming into contact with the business. I have walked into the offices of potential customers to look at training and can sense it (it's always a good sign if a company is investing in customer service training anyway!) One such company is Stena Line, a brilliant example of how to create the 'wow' culture.

▶ brilliant example

Stena Line has an outstanding reputation for the quality and delivery of its service. The company carries over three million passengers on its Irish Sea routes each year, more than its rival ferry operators combined. Its strategy of a rolling investment programme, which over the last 10 years has included £150 million on the Irish Sea route alone, has been matched by its commitment to customer service.

The Route Director, Head of On Board Services and Head of Training have changed the culture through inspiring, motivating and listening to their people.

Their ethos is simple yet effective – happy staff makes happy customers which gives happy financials.

As the Route Director, emphasised: 'Communication is key' and it is so important to 'build the staff's trust'.

Initially, when Stena Line started out on its journey of transforming the organisation from a traditional ferry operation to a customer service organisation, staff were asked to identify where Stena currently stood and what needed to change to make Stena Line become one of the best companies in the world. Employees were listened to and their ideas acted on.

All ships' staff are empowered to resolve a customer complaint up to 1,000 euros. This has rarely been used but staff feel valued and trusted that they have the authority to use this if they feel it is appropriate.

Recognition has played a big part in developing the culture of the company. Ideas include:

● hand-written note of thanks from the Route Director;
● acknowledging staff birthdays, anniversaries and family occasions;
● WOW vouchers;
● Service Excellence awards;
● Values Champions.

What I really like about the Stena Line example is how everyone is involved from the senior director and managers and the front-line team. They have total support and commitment from senior managers, yet the front-line staff have created and delivered the initiatives. The result is a team which feels empowered and motivated, and the knock-on effect for the customer is lots of smiling, engaging individuals making their experience enjoyable and memorable. This has really helped Stena through a very difficult trading period with very stiff competition. If it had just focused on the quality of the vessels and the cost of the trips, it would not be in the position it is in now, ready to make the most of the improvement in the economy.

brilliant recap

- Always be aware of the emotional scale and how your customers are feeling. Remember, we are moving into a customer-experience economy rather than a customer-satisfaction economy.

- Identify moments of truth in your business or in the part you work in. Look at them through the customers' eyes and experience them as they do so that you can make any necessary changes.

- Turn as many of your moments of truth into 'wow' moments even if they are negative to start with; this will push your customers up the emotional scale towards the good feeling place, where they are more forgiving of any failings or mistakes you make.

- Look for bad moments of truth and eliminate them from the customers' experience.

- Are you a good-feeling business or a bad-feeling business? What are you doing to build on your current offering and what have you got to do to improve the experience for the customer?

- Motivate and manage your customer service team to create passion, energy and commitment to your strategy of achieving a good-feeling business culture.

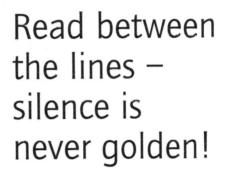

CHAPTER 5

Read between the lines – silence is never golden!

Probably the hardest job is convincing people employed in customer service roles that complaining customers are a good thing. It's an accepted part of the job but the least enjoyable. Seeing complaints through a positive-coloured filter, where they are valuable and helpful to a business, really helps; positively satisfying a customer's complaint makes them feel better too. If you have a strong process for encouraging complaints, dealing with them, ultimately reviewing and changing the business because of them, they suddenly become incredible opportunities and the most important moment of truth of all.

Silence, the deadly killer of your business

Amazingly, many businesses evaluate their customer service strategy by the number of complaints they get. 'We have very few complaints from our customers, so we don't need customer service training at the moment.' I am told this regularly when prospecting for new clients. Either that or, 'The number of complaints has dramatically decreased this year and we are very pleased, it seems our customer service initiatives are working'. Companies using this type of measure are in denial. Although it is tempting to bury your head in the sand and believe no news is good news, trust me, if customers are not complaining to you, then they are complaining to other people or they are just never using your business again. The concerning thing is that customers who don't complain there and then increasingly

there are lots of
statistics to prove that
silence isn't golden

post their views on the Internet and through the social networking sites; they are no longer telling nine or so people but are probably telling thousands!

There are lots of statistics to prove that silence isn't golden; the following are just a few of them:

- For every customer who bothers to complain, there are 26 others who will remain silent (Lee Resources Inc.).

- Research shows that around 96% of customers don't complain when they have a problem – they just don't come back. Since only 4% of unhappy customers complain, you could make the mistake of assuming that nothing is wrong with your business.

- The annual Service in Britain survey found half the population said they would rather take their business elsewhere than complain, and a similar proportion said that they wanted to complain but didn't because it involved too much effort.

- Unhappy customers tell at least nine other people.

- 65% of an average company's business comes from presently satisfied customers.

At the risk of repetition, we need to look through a different filter. Instead of seeing complaints as a reflection of bad service, it's much better to see them as a reflection of how much your customer cares, wanting to remain loyal to your business! Be grateful for complaints, a complaining customer is doing what many companies hire consultants and mystery shoppers to do – critique the service and then give feedback to shape the way we conduct our business in future.

Do you or your company welcome and encourage your customers to complain? Are you able to handle feedback in a non-defensive fashion? Have you made the process of getting feedback from the customer simple and easy? Do you listen intently to what they have to say, correct the problem and then follow up with your appreciation? Do you then look for ways to improve yourself or your business, so the customer experience is improved? If you don't do all of these things, you will be losing business.

Ways in which complaints are discouraged

● When it is vague about to whom or where customers should address their complaints.

● The customer is passed round, with no one taking responsibility.

● Limited or no follow-up with the customer.

● The complaint handling is started by asking for irrelevant information.

● When the complaint handler's body language and overall attitude suggest that they don't want to hear the complaint.

● Not listening to the customers.

● Denial or not accepting that there is a problem or that problems don't normally happen.

● Using rigid policy.

● Setting goals to reduce complaints.

● Blaming the customer and getting defensive.

● Phone systems that make customers wait.

Actually, it's the customers who don't complain that you have to worry about – the ones who don't feel like expending energy to confront you or write a letter or who are not bold enough to tell you what they are unhappy with. They slip quietly away never to be seen again and statistically tell nine other people. It's brilliant though, by actively encouraging customers to complain and dealing with them well, not only can you retain them but they also become advocates, and what better way to increase business?

Why don't customers complain?

A good starting point for answering this question is to ask yourself when you last complained (if ever). What happened when you complained? How did you feel? At each point, where did you register on the emotional scale, and where were you emotionally at the end of the experience? If you never complain, why not? Really reflecting on your own emotions when complaining can help you get an insight into the customers and how they feel.

---

brilliant example

A friend of mine was travelling with 12 companions on a well known airline, and six hours into the ten-hour flight they still had not been fed. They complained to each other, but none of them said anything to the crew as they didn't want to make a fuss. However, in the end, overcome by hunger, one of the party volunteered to make the complaint. The crew member was called and the volunteer very politely, said 'I am so sorry to bother you but could you please tell us when we might get some food; it's been six hours and we are all really hungry'. The crew member looked straight at him and said, 'So is Africa!'

It's hard to believe this reaction, and when treated like this it is no wonder that customers are reluctant to complain or give us any critical feedback. Here are some of the reasons why we don't complain.

● We are taught from a very early age that complaining is negative and we should just get on with it.

● We think someone else will do it so there is no need to bother.

- We don't want to stand out and prefer to be unobtrusive.
- We have a fear of confrontation and conflict.
- We have had bad experiences of complaining in the past.
- We just don't have the time for it.
- We don't think anything will change or be done about it anyway.
- It's just too much hassle.
- It makes us feel bad.
- We don't actually know how we can make a complaint.

One reason from the above list states that customers don't complain because, having tried in the past, they haven't gotten much satisfaction from the experience. What is your expectation when you complain? Is it that someone will listen patiently? Not be defensive, apologise, solve your problem and take time to say thank you? I bet it isn't. We all have memories of not being taken seriously or ignored or made to feel a nuisance. The truth is that complaining takes us to the wrong end of the emotional scale, to the bad-feeling place. If you are having a good-feeling experience shopping and an opportunity arises to complain, the chances are that you would rather stay in the good-feeling place. Rather than get close up and personal with the problem, you ignore it and then moan like mad about it later.

In Chapter 2 on cornerstones of customer service we looked at different types of customers based on their behavioural preferences. This also impacts on how they approach a problem.

- **The red customer**. These customers are the most likely to complain. They are direct, honest and believe in giving feedback on the spot. They are not so concerned about hurting people's feelings, usually having no fear of confrontation. On the other hand, they are task-focused and want things done quickly; if the process is long-winded and takes too long, they will lose patience and won't come back.

- **The yellow customer.** They are motivated by being liked and popular. They absolutely hate complaining, especially if it's directly to the person causing them to. Any sort of personal confrontation will make them extremely uncomfortable. Chances are they won't say anything there and then but will use it as a great story to tell at dinner parties. They will probably tell more people than any of the other types. If they do complain and are made to feel bad, they will be lost as a customer for ever.

- **The green customer.** Of all the types, they are in the main pleasers; they look for the best in everything and everyone. They probably keep going back to a business and giving it a second and a third chance just to be fair. They never complain, but eventually get disheartened and give up. If encouraged to complain and made to feel good, they would become a customer for life.

- **The blue customer.** They don't have a problem with actually complaining, but in how they complain. They don't want to do it personally and like to be able to consider all of the facts so they can be clear and objective in their feedback. They are the ones who are most likely to be discouraged by a lack of acknowledgement about the time spent to write/send feedback. They need to know it's been taken seriously.

The secrets to encouraging complaints

It sounds simple, but the secret is to keep customers in the good-feeling place on the emotional scale. There are various ways to do this and it can be different depending on their behavioural type. Here are some key suggestions.

Make it easy for them to complain

If it's decided that we want more complaints, then it should be made easy for customers to voice their opinions in the best way to suit their type. Ironically, I spent a week writing this book at my health club, during which I received the worst service from the café there that I have ever experienced, and I was struck by how difficult it was to complain. It caused such a fuss and no one seemed to know what to do that I decided to work in another well known coffee shop the following week. They were unable to get the feedback they needed to keep a customer's loyalty; if it's not made easy, you will fall at the first hurdle. Secondly, when a customer has decided to make a complaint, and they run into hurdles and barriers trying to voice their problems, all that happens is that they get angrier and angrier and further along the emotional scale to the bad-feeling place, resulting in a small problem developing into a much larger one, simply because the customer cannot find a way to channel their concerns, anger, fears, worries, questions or complaints to your organisation in a timely and convenient manner.

brilliant tips

How to make it easy

- However the complaint comes, welcome it. Don't react in a defensive way or try to push the blame back on the customer. (How to do this is covered in the chapter on handling complaints.)
- Deal with it quickly and take it seriously; make the customer feel important.
- Don't get caught up in complicated processes which confuse the customer. Keep it simple.
- Keep it personal. Even if the complaints come through a website, make the acknowledgement of the complaint as personal as possible.
- Have several options on how customers can complain to apply to different personality types, such as face to face, feedback

▶

cards, by email, etc. The UK Customer Service Institute (UKCSI) reported that 46% prefer to telephone; 18% prefer email.

● Don't hide your customer complaints/information department. It's amazing how many large retail outlets do this! According to the UKCSI, 29% of customers don't know how to complain, or who to complain to.

● Take responsibility – if you can, deal with the complaint first hand. Customers hate having to be called back or even having to speak to a manager – it just builds on the uncomfortable feelings they have already experienced.

● Publish how they can complain and that you encourage and act on feedback.

Thank them for complaining

We need to let our customers know that they will always be heard, listened to and taken seriously. Now we see complaints as positive and the customers who complain as loyal and trying to help, it's common sense then to thank, reward and appreciate them for complaining. This could be as simple as saying 'thank you' or it could be some sort of reward scheme. A lot of airlines have prize draws for free holidays for customers who fill in feedback questionnaires.

▶ brilliant example

On a recent business trip to Malaysia I experienced a great example of appreciation for complaining. After walking all over the city trying to find a decent restaurant, we were really pleased to find one which was absolutely beautiful inside. However, I wasn't very happy about my meal. It was so salty I just couldn't eat it and, as it was getting late, I decided to leave it and say nothing. When the waiter returned to check that everything was

OK, he noticed I hadn't touched the food on my plate. He asked in a very concerned way if there was anything wrong, and being typically British, I don't like to complain, but when asked directly I could do nothing else but explain the reason for not eating it. He seemed really quite distressed and, even though I said it was OK and I didn't want anything else, he returned a few minutes later with the manager, who then went on to thank me for my feedback as this was a new restaurant and they were really keen to get things right. He told me that he had informed the chef about my feedback. He assured me he would adjust the seasoning next time he made the dish.

This in itself made me feel so much better about complaining; I was right back up the emotional scale, and then to top it all, the waiter brought out a platter of desserts with a sample of everything from the menu. He explained that it was 'on the house' and they would really value our feedback. The desserts were delicious and we were delighted. We went back to our hotel and recommended the restaurant to everyone.

The key to this example is how it made me feel. On the emotional scale I went from fear of confrontation to uncomfortable and then to appreciation and feeling important and then finally to advocate.

Be proactive

We want more complaints, so we have to be proactive rather than reactive. Most businesses react to complaints; they don't dig them out. The impact dissatisfied customers have on your business can be devastating. If you want to be brilliant, seek out and deal with every unhappy customer. Your potential for success will increase with every complaint you find! Asking for is better than responding to complaints but only after customers are brave enough to voice their issues.

> if you want to be brilliant, seek out and deal with every unhappy customer

brilliant tips

How to ask for complaints

- If you deal with long-term customers, after finishing a project, ask for a meeting; tell them you've been thrilled to have their business, and you're working very hard to build a business with the highest level of customer service possible. Then ask:
  - 'How did we do?'
  - 'How could we have done better?'
  - 'If you were me, what else would you have done?'

- When seeking feedback asking questions like, 'Are you happy with everything?' won't get you anything useful. When we get asked this type of question, say, in a restaurant, we nearly always say 'Yes, fine', even if it's not. You need to specifically ask for a complaint: 'We really value customer feedback. What can we do to improve your experience?', then leave some silence. This will encourage your customer to think and respond. Of course, you also need to use your best focused listening.

- If you observe something wrong, don't ignore it; see it as an opportunity to build customer loyalty and get feedback. Like my example of the waiter in the restaurant, if he had just taken my food away and said nothing, the lasting experience would have been bad.

- Comment cards. Provide brief, half-page comment cards on which they can answer basic questions: 'Were you satisfied with our services?'; 'How could we provide the perfect services?'; 'Are there any services you'd like to see that don't exist yet?' Again, if possible, take these to the customers and ask them to complete them, explaining how important they are to enable you to deliver brilliant service. One of my customers, Stena Line, encourages staff to go round with the cards and get them completed while they wait; they have large bags of sweets to give away at the same time, and it creates an opportunity for them to interact with the customers at the end of a trip and get genuine feedback.

- Surveys by mail/email. You might hate answering these, but plenty of people don't – and they will fill out surveys, especially if they get something in return. Promise them a discount or offer if they return the completed form to your business.

- Telephone surveys. These can be really useful if you do them with the attitude we mentioned previously where you want critical feedback not just lip-service compliments.

- Customer events. Depending on your business, find ways to be in contact with your customers – dinners, lunches, seminars and any type of corporate hospitality.

- Online communities. Create chat boards, message rooms, email discussion, anything that encourages your customers to communicate, and then monitor these regularly.

- Focus groups. These can be a fantastic way of involving your customers in the success of your business; they create brilliant ideas, build relationships and encourage honest feedback. If you reward your customers for taking part, it also makes them feel important and appreciated.

- Front-line staff. If you are a manager, listen to your staff. They deal with complaints first hand and can give you valuable information. By involving them they also feel motivated and empowered.

Making complaints count

As mentioned earlier, one reason we don't complain is that we think nothing will change, so what's the point. If customers could see that the company not only welcomes the feedback, but

one reason we don't
complain is that we
think nothing will
change

makes changes as a result, wouldn't
that be the ultimate reward for
taking the trouble to complain? The
perfect scenario is the customers
feeding back to the front-line staff,
the front-line staff feeding back to
the management/business owners and then this filtering back
into the company's culture in the form of improved/brilliant
service. If there is a way to share this policy with your customers,
it is the best way of encouraging them to complain. The reward
for the customers is that they get better service and they feel
better about the relationship with the company.

brilliant tip

If you are a manager or a business owner, get out and watch your
customers at the point of service. Spend time watching, listening to
or interacting with actual customers. Use the information to create
a service recovery policy that feeds back into your business.

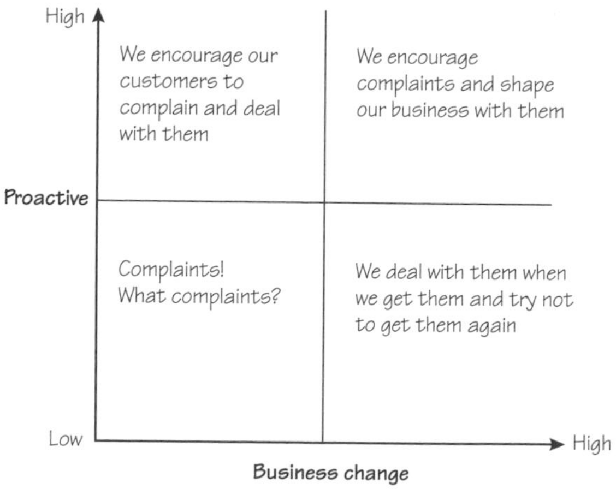

Figure 5.1 The service-recovery matrix

If you look at the matrix in Figure 5.1, where is your company? And what can you do to move it into the top right quadrant?

The professional complainers

After looking at complaints in a totally positive way, there are some customers who just complain and complain and complain. They are professional complainers and no matter what you do, they never seem to be satisfied. In fact, they don't want to be satisfied and frustrate everyone, including other customers. If you spend too much time with these people, you have less time to implement a positive service recovery system, or less time with other customers.

brilliant tip

Dealing with professional complainers

- First of all, acknowledge that there aren't that many of them. Don't let them persuade you to view all complainers through the same filter.

- Isolate professional complainers from your other customers and, if you can, from your business.

- Never accept abusive behaviour and refuse to deal with anyone if they adopt these behaviours.

- A well known chain of restaurants has a policy of three complaints (this is not necessarily a good measure), and then they politely inform the customer that they are very sorry but they are unable to meet their expectations and suggest they might prefer a different restaurant. In other words, pass them on to your competition!

- Finally, and most importantly, don't let these customers take what they really want from you – which is more and more of your precious time and attention.

More complaints = more business

If you are a manager of a customer service or a business owner, here is a reminder of why you need to implement a service-recovery process:

- Research shows that it costs five times more to get a new customer than it does to keep a current one. Getting new clients creates a buzz and expend a lot of energy. Maintaining our current customers seems, on the face of it, less exciting, but it's vital if you want to grow your business.

Sales without customer service is like stuffing money into a pocket full of holes.

David Tooman

- Customer loyalty is higher after a complaint has been successfully resolved, and creates the most important moments of truth; customers are more likely to recommend your business upon a positive outcome.

- An excellent service-recovery policy gives you a good name and your reputation is enhanced. Not having a policy leaves you open to a damaged reputation.

- Whenever a customer buys a product or a service, there's a risk attached. If they experience a complaint and it's handled well, the risk of buying from you again is reduced. Companies that offer a money back guarantee and mean it are creating a feeling of security, making it easy for the customer to buy. On the emotional scale of buying, peace of mind is very important.

- Dealing with complaints costs money. If you listen to your customers and use their feedback to eliminate problems and improve your business, complaints will be reduced, ultimately saving you money.

- Complaining customers are a huge demotivator for

customer service people. Seeing these customers as gifts, learning to view them more positively and being shown how to deal with them more effectively will allow them to have a more positive attitude. They will witness the positive effects on the business, helping with staff retention, again saving the business money.

brilliant recap

- Don't see a lack of complaints as a good thing; it is not a way to measure customer satisfaction.

- View complaints as gifts. They build loyalty, give you valuable feedback and bring you more business.

- Understand why customers don't complain to give you a valuable insight into their emotions and how they feel. Consider their personality type and be flexible with your procedures.

- Make it easy to complain.

- Genuinely appreciate and thank your customers for their complaints; they are trying to help you and the business.

- Be proactive. Encourage and seek out feedback. Find ways to allow your customers to be honest.

- Act on the feedback and let your customers know they are helping to shape the way you and your company work.

- Control your professional complainers and support staff when necessary.

- Remember, complaints = business.

This chapter has been about welcoming complaints and changing our attitude to them. If we don't deal with complaints correctly, they can become very negative moments for all. The next chapter looks at the best way to handle all types of complaint to complete the service-recovery process.

CHAPTER 6

How to handle *any* complaint

I f our policy is not just to welcome complaints but actively encourage them, then we have to be experts on handling them so we can turn them into 'wow' moments of truth to use as opportunities to build customer loyalty. We know that for many reasons most customers don't complain – it can make them feel bad and puts them at the wrong end of the emotional scale. Think about it as if you were the customer. Firstly, you have a complaint which must mean you are not happy about something. You could be anywhere on the emotional scale from mildly irritated to extremely angry, and complaining only makes it worse. You can now add embarrassment or even fear to the mix and despite all of these feelings, you then make your complaint and are met with disinterest, blame, lack of trust or even rudeness. I am not sure we have an emotional scale long enough to record how the customer could feel.

> think about it as if you were the customer

From a business point of view, we also need to be aware of how we feel when faced with an upset or angry customer. What filter are we looking at them through? This can have a major impact on how we deal with them in that moment. If we are having a bad day for any reason, this could cause us to be impatient with or irritated by a complaining customer.

In this chapter we are also going to look at you and how you react so that you can be more aware of your behaviours and reactions. In my training workshops, I encourage customer service staff to be aware of their default position, in other words, the place they go when they are under pressure. Even the nicest, most rational people can find they have physical reactions to a very angry customer, so it's important to have some strategies to deal with these so that you are in the right frame of mind to respond to the customer in the most positive way.

We are going to start with the most challenging situations where the customer is upset and angry as this gives us a good foundation from which to look at any complaints. Keep in mind the following statistics as a way to remind yourself how important it is to have complaints and listen to angry customers prepared to tell you how they feel; it will help to see any situation through a positive filter:

- 70% of complaining customers will do business with you again if you resolve the complaint in their favour. (Source: Lee Resources Inc.)

- 95% of complaining customers will do business with you again if you resolve the complaint instantly. (Source: Lee Resources Inc.)

- Reducing customer defections can boost profits by 25–85%. In 73% of cases, the organisation made no attempt to persuade dissatisfied customers to stay; even though 35% said that a simple apology would have prevented them from moving to the competition. (Source: NOP.)

Dealing with very angry customers

It starts with you.

To be an expert at handling complaints you will need all of the interpersonal skills we looked at in Chapter 2. These skills are your main toolkit and they are even more important when you are dealing with more difficult situations. The challenge is that when we get upset the things we need to be doing are the hardest things to do. We find ourselves interrupting instead of listening or blaming instead of empathising. We need to remain assertive even if the customer is being aggressive.

Understanding assertive behaviour

brilliant definitions

Aggressive

Putting your rights and needs before others'

Passive

Allowing others' rights and needs before yours.

Assertive

To respect the personal rights and needs of others whilst maintaining your own rights and needs in a reasonable and responsible manner.

Assertive behaviour is often confused with aggressive behaviour, but you can see from the above definitions that they are very different. The key element is the ability to understand someone else's rights and needs first and if you need to defuse someone else's aggressive behaviour this makes complete sense. The reason it can be challenging is that our natural behaviours are either passive or aggressive and invoke our fight or flight responses. Our ancestors needed these responses to ensure survival. If you were walking through a meadow and a huge hairy mammoth came charging towards you, your choice would either be to run and hide (flight/passive) or stand and fight (fight/aggressive). You definitely would not try to listen and reason with a charging mammoth. We still experience these reactions in our modern world even though we don't have hairy mammoths to contend with. When we are in a situation where the customer is angry and aggressive, our body will react to it because it is a stressful situation. This means we physically prepare for an urgent response to threat. This results in increased adrenalin going to the front part of our brain. Our bodies are getting ready for the extreme physical exertion of either fighting or running for our lives. If we don't actually need to do this, the adrenalin can make us feel very uncomfortable and affect our behaviour.

Fight/flight response – what is happening to me?

● A rise in temperature, feeling flushed, even breaking out in a sweat.

● Breathlessness.

● The heart beating faster/palpitations.

● Muscle tension and shaking.

● Restlessness and fidgeting.

● Swallowing from increases in saliva.

These reactions result in our natural judgement being suspended because the fight and flight responses are all about action and that's what we are preparing for. This means we are more impulsive; we have racing thoughts and it can lead us to behave aggressively in a way we may totally regret later, or we can retreat and avoid taking any responsibility. All in all, none of this is helpful when dealing with angry and upset customers. Of course, they are also reacting from the same set of responses and this can give us some clues on how to deal with them if we can keep our own behaviour in check.

What is your default position?

Before we look at ways to minimise the effect of these physical responses, it's a good idea to have an understanding of which behaviour you are most likely to adopt, aggressive or passive.

This can then help you to be aware of what you are doing and adopt strategies to push through the behaviours.

Fill in the questionnaire below honestly and it will give you an indication of your most likely reaction.

Think about your behaviour at work and circle the score which best typifies you.

4 = Always

3 = Often

2 = Seldom

1 = Never

Be honest! There are no right or wrong answers.

1   When I am not happy about a situation,
    I drop hints to other people about my feelings.   4 3 2 1

2   If I realise the person to whom I am talking is
    not listening, I dry up.   4 3 2 1

3   When I am not sure how to undertake a task,
    I feel at ease asking for assistance.   4 3 2 1

4   When someone does not agree with what I am
    saying, I raise my voice to make my point.   4 3 2 1

5   I feel embarrassed when someone
    compliments me.   4 3 2 1

6   I let my boss know when I disagree with him
    or her.   4 3 2 1

7   I like to be in control of a situation.   4 3 2 1

8   When someone takes advantage of me, I find
    a way to even the score.   4 3 2 1

9   When I disagree with someone, I give them
    the silent treatment.   4 3 2 1

10   I feel guilty when I have to ask others for help.   4 3 2 1

11   I express my opinion to others in an honest
     and direct way when it is appropriate to do so.   4 3 2 1

12   I vocalise my frustration loudly and strongly
     when I don't get my way.   4 3 2 1

13   If I don't agree with a task that I have been
     given, I find a way of dragging my feet over it.   4 3 2 1

14   I prefer to comply with the majority decision
     even if it is not convenient for me.   4 3 2 1

Now score how strongly you agree with the following statements, where:

4   = Agree strongly

3   = Agree somewhat

2   = Disagree somewhat

1   = Disagree strongly

15   I am confident in expressing my position/claim.   4 3 2 1

16   I don't like telling people my honest opinion
     if I think it will hurt their feelings.   4 3 2 1

17   I believe it is important not to 'rock the boat'.   4 3 2 1

18   I am not afraid of what others think of me.   4 3 2 1

19   My anger tends to be explosive.   4 3 2 1

20   I don't mind offending people if it means
     getting my message across.   4 3 2 1

How to score

Now enter the score that you have given to each statement in the appropriate box below. Then total each of the columns downwards.

S.1	S.2	S.3	S.4
S.8	S.5	S.6	S.7
S.9	S.10	S.11	S.12
S.13	S.14	S.15	S.19
S.16	S.17	S.18	S.20
Total	Total	Total	Total
Passive aggressive	Passive	Assertive	Aggressive

Look at the column where your score is the highest. This is the behaviour that is typical of you most of the time. Assertiveness is often the highest score for people who work in customer services because they work hard at learning these behaviours. The important score is your second highest. This is your default style, the behaviour you adopt when you are under pressure or are stressed.

If your first and second highest scores are similar, this indicates that you can adopt either style, dependent upon the situation. You may even have three or four scores that are similar – this would indicate that you have learnt to use several behavioural styles.

Understanding the behaviours

The four main styles are outlined below. It is important to recognise that these styles do not necessarily describe a person but their behaviour at a particular time.

Passive behaviour

Often caused by a lack of self-esteem and confidence, passive behaviour involves avoiding stating needs or opinions or by doing so in an apologetic manner. For example, 'I don't have the experience to deal with that. I will have to put you through to my manager...' or 'I hope you don't mind me saying, but...' Other examples include simply not stating that you have a preference or not giving your views, which may well be valid.

Passive behaviour may be caused by a desire to please and to avoid conflict but its effect is often the opposite. It can seem to customers that the customer service assistant is not taking responsibility and it can come over as weak and ineffectual. This has a tendency to be irritating or frustrating and, ironically, can make the customer angrier.

Aggressive behaviour

Although aggressive behaviour may involve anger, shouting, and so forth, this is not necessarily so. Any behaviour which contravenes the rights of others is aggressive. For example, interrupting the customer when they are trying to explain the situation or taking a contrary position without appreciating the other side. A more devious example would be someone who is acting calm and adopts a patronising tone when attempting to placate a customer.

People often do not realise that they are behaving aggressively. A high level of self-confidence can lead someone to dominate without realising the effect of their behaviour on others. Indeed, a lack of confidence may be hidden by a brash exterior and an individual will find it hard to believe they are perceived as being aggressive when feeling 'knotted up' inside.

Passive aggressive behaviour

Passive aggressive behaviour is probably the most destructive behaviour of all. It is where we retreat and adopt passive behaviour towards the customer and then, once the confrontation is over, we either keep thinking about it or go around moaning about it to anyone who will listen.

Passive aggressive is:

Like taking a spoon full of poison and expecting the other person to die.

Anonymous

Assertive behaviour

Assertive behaviour is based on honesty. It is a clear statement of needs, feelings and opinions, said directly without apology. This is balanced by sensitivity to, and respect for, the rights of others.

Passive	Aggressive	Assertive
● Afraid to speak up	● Interrupts and talks over	● Listens and allows the other person space to speak
● Speaking softly/ mumbling	● Loud voice/shouting	
	● Too much direct eye contact/staring	
● Avoids eye contact		● Speaks openly
● Shows little expression	● Intimidating expressions	● Good eye contact
● Crouched body language, trying to look small or invisible	● Negative body language, pointing, invading personal space	● Expressions that match the message
		● Relaxed and open body language
● Making promises they can't or won't keep	● Only interested in own needs and rights	● Shows empathy and consideration for another point of view
● Not taking responsibility/passing the buck	● Blames and defends	
		● Negotiates joint solutions

brilliant dos and don'ts

Controlling the fight or flight response

Do

✔ Be in the moment. When you are 'in the moment' your mind is not racing ahead filling itself with all sorts of concerns about what might or could happen. Instead you are focused on dealing with the customer at that moment. It will help to stop your thoughts getting more and more negative which increases the level of stress. Our brains can't distinguish between real danger and stress caused from our overreaction. Also, you are alert and responsive and more likely to respond in the right way. Trust yourself to say the right thing at the right time and go with the flow.

▶

✔ Stand up if possible. If you are dealing with an angry customer on the telephone, it can really help to release tension if you stand up. Take deep breaths whenever possible. If you can't stand, be sure to sit 'square' in your seat. Uncross your legs. Place your feet on the floor, straighten your back and let your arms rest comfortably in your lap.

✔ Take a reality check. In the midst of a challenging situation irrational fears may take over, often quite without foundation. Remind yourself that this is your natural fight/flight response kicking in; you have dealt successfully with similar situations in the past; take confidence from that.

✔ Stay focused on a positive outcome. Remind yourself that what you are doing is vital to your success and the success of the business.

Don't

✘ Hold your breath. This sounds too simple and too obvious but even in role-play situations I have seen customer service people holding their breath when dealing with an angry customer. When we're extremely anxious we tend either to hold our breath or breathe very shallowly off the top of our lungs. The result is that we prolong and heighten the physical discomfort brought on by acute anxiety.

✘ Take it personally. It's important not to detach from the customer but don't take their anger personally. Remember they are responding to their own natural responses and are not thinking rationally.

Turning angry to advocate

You now have an understanding of what happens when you are under stress from an angry customer. Now we need to step into their shoes and understand how they feel. Because you are calm and thinking rationally you can use the following ideas to move them along the emotional scale from angry to an advocate and they will be more loyal to you and your company than before they had the problem.

Acknowledge the anger

It's a big mistake for customer service people to ignore the anger. If you think about when you are angry, you expect people to respond to it, otherwise you think you're not getting through to them and you get angrier. When a customer is angry, they are trying to communicate with you; they are starting a chain of communication; a failure to respond to communication leaves the communication unlinked ... broken. For example, if you meet someone and say 'Good morning what a lovely day' and they don't look at you or say anything, the communication chain is broken. If you don't acknowledge their form of communication, i.e. the anger, they could resort to whatever it takes to feel heard and understood.

You can keep your angry customers from getting angrier by assertively acknowledging their anger and responding to it. Try a statement like, 'I can see you're upset and I want you to know that getting to the bottom of this is really important to me'. This statement directly and professionally addresses anger – without making the customer even angrier. Now that the anger has been acknowledged, you have completed the communication chain and the customer feels heard and respected.

Let the anger run out of steam

A very angry customer is a bit like a volcano when it erupts: you cannot stop it once it starts and you can't plug it up. It also erupts at its own pace. You can't make it hurry up. You can't even get it to change direction – you just have to let it erupt. When a customer is angry, they must experience and express their anger – and often this

> when a customer is angry, they must experience and express their anger

is done through ranting. Don't interrupt an angry ranting customer or tell them to 'calm down'. This would be as pointless as trying to stop a volcano (on average most customers won't rant for much longer than 35 seconds). Just like a volcano, the customer will run out of steam and they are then in a position to hear what you have to say. So use all of your focused listening techniques so that the customer feels they are being heard.

Appreciate and apologise

It's amazing the effect the words 'thank you for telling us and I'm sorry this has happened' can have. If we go back to the emotional scale again, when someone says sorry and means it, it takes us to empathy for them and then forgiveness. This takes the customer to a place where they start to feel they are in partnership with you. Whether the fault lies with the customer OR the company, always apologise. If you are worried about accepting responsibility for something that's not your fault, use some of the tips below of how you can apologise safely and sincerely.

brilliant tips

Apologising without admitting liability

'Please accept my apology for any inconvenience this misunderstanding may have caused you.'

'I am really sorry that you have had to bring this to our attention.'

'I am sorry you're in this position.'

Notice that these apologies do not blame the company or the customer ... they are offered simply to create goodwill. Always apologise and be sure that your tone and body language send the same message.

Provide an explanation

This is important because we do like to know why something has happened, so it's important to provide an explanation for how or why the problem happened. Taking time to explain to a customer what might have caused the problem helps to re-establish trust. Keep it simple and quick and stick to the facts. Don't slip into over-justification or even blame other parts of the business. It does have to come after 'appreciate and apologise', otherwise it will look like an excuse. Something like this is ideal:

'Thanks for taking the time to let us know about _____. We appreciate customers who let us know when things aren't right. Here's what we think may have happened...'

Seek to understand

Acting assertively means that we seek to understand first, so the point at which the anger is running out of steam is a good time to offer some genuine empathy. This is the time to focus on the person complaining and not the complaint. Then move on to asking questions, probing to increase your understanding of the problem, reflect back your interpretation of their issue without judgements to test your assumptions and keep any blame or defensiveness out of it.

Building and blocking language

Be aware of your use of language when delivering empathic statements. We often have a tendency to say something like, 'I totally understand why you are so upset. If I had waited as long for my meal I would be the same...' and then comes the word BUT 'we are really busy today'. So what are we saying with the BUT? We are saying that we don't really understand why they are upset at all; we are completely undoing all the good work with the empathic statement. This is called *blocking language* because it creates a block between us and the customer; what we need to use is *building language*.

For example:

- 'The girl was beautiful BUT she was tall.' The real meaning is that the girl wasn't beautiful at all because blocking language is being used.

- 'The girl was beautiful AND tall.' This is an example of how building language builds on the positive.

Blocking language is a form of aggressive behaviour and can be a subconscious reaction to how you are feeling. If your default behaviour is aggressive, you will be more likely to slip into this language, and it is a bad habit to use the BUT word. When running exercises in my training workshops we work on eliminating the word when dealing with upset customers and we are told by customer service people that it's one of the hardest things to do.

it is a bad habit to use the BUT word

Building language acknowledges and builds on what has been said. It adds to the feeling of being heard and understood. Customer service people who use more building language have a better chance of defusing potentially emotional situations, which are more likely to reach positive conclusions. Whereas if too much blocking language is used, this can cause more argument and the customer feels they are just being shut up and not being really understood.

Blocking language	Building language
But...	And...
However...	What I would add is...
Actually (tone of voice) ...	Equally...
Although...	I also...
Nonetheless...	In addition...
Yet...	Have you thought... (question)
What you don't understand is...	Another point is...
What you need to understand is...	I think...

Examples of building language

'I totally understand *and*...'

'I appreciate how frustrating this has been. *What I would add* to that is...'

'I take your point *and equally* I would like to add...'

'You have a really good point. *In addition* to that *I also* need to ask...'

'I take your point about "X". (*Pause*) Can I suggest...'

'I see...what is your feeling on...?'

brilliant tip

If you are worried about using too much blocking language and building language seems unnatural and awkward, then simply leave a pause before you go on to say anything or ask a question.

Take responsibility

Now that you have totally understood the customer's issues, it's really important to take responsibility. One emotion customers often feel when they complain is one of powerlessness; they don't know what the response will be, whether they will be understood or if anything will be done. To alleviate this feeling for the customer, a great technique is to ask what it will take to meet their needs or to satisfy them. Or, alternatively, make some suggestions that are related to their problem and ask which solution is the most acceptable. This puts them back in control and improves their emotional response. One of the great things about receiving complaints is that it gives us a second chance to solve the problem and restore the customer's confidence. Whatever is agreed, see it through to the end. This is a crucial time in the moment of truth. If the customer leaves you here and the solution you have agreed does not happen or goes wrong, all the good work you have done will have been for nothing.

🔘 brilliant example

As I mentioned earlier, I spent a week writing this book in the café at my health club (where I have been a member of for nearly seven years) and received really bad service. One lunch time we were told we would have to wait for 45 minutes for our food because they were very busy. This in itself didn't go down well but after nearly an hour we asked if we were going to get the food and were informed that the order had not been put through and we would have to wait another 20 minutes. If I hadn't had my laptop all set up, I would have gone somewhere else, but we stuck with it. When the food finally arrived it was really bad so we complained to the waiter. He was definitely in a passive default position because he could hardly look at us and went and got the manager. The manager did a fantastic job of listening to our complaint, thanking us and then he said he would give us a refund for the whole meal. He really turned it round, and we were back up the emotional scale and actually feeling quite sorry for them being so busy. But when we came to leave we realised that we had not had the refund. The manager was nowhere to be seen and my husband had the humiliating task of going to the front of a busy queue to explain everything and to finally get the refund. We left the club, irritated, humiliated and disappointed, not where you want a customer to be when it has cost you time and money to resolve the problem. All the manager had to do was see it through to the end and this example would have been a different one. Figure 6.1 illustrates the process of taking responsibility for a complaint.

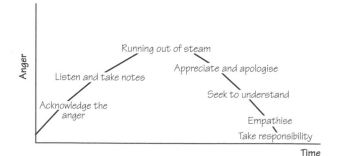

Figure 6.1 Climbing the mountain of anger

brilliant tips

When it becomes abusive

Sometimes customers can totally lose it and they become abusive, or they might start the call in abusive mode. Abusive is defined as verbally threatening, using foul language and emotionally out of control. When you have used all of the previous techniques and procedures and the customer becomes abusive, or if the customer begins the conversation in an abusive manner, it's time to use some advanced strategies for managing the customer's behaviour. It's also time to protect yourself. It's more likely the customer will become abusive with telephone customer service reps, as the contact is more anonymous.

Here are some steps you can take to manage the out of control customer.

1   **Bring it back to the personal.** The less personal the interaction, the more likely it can get out of control. As soon as you feel the customer's anger might go out of control, and you've tried everything and nothing works, it's time to use the 'personalise the conversation' strategy. Call the customer by name, and refer to their company by name. Restate your name, and remind them that (your company name) wants them to be satisfied.

2   **Remind them you are on their side** and that you want to solve the problem. Let them know you can solve the problem only when the language is appropriate, and demands are reasonable. You should never allow the customer to continue if they're using inappropriate language, or if they're totally out of control. Nothing will be accomplished, and they'll sabotage your efforts to stay composed. They'll lose respect for you and the company for allowing the situation to continue. If they cannot maintain enough control to conduct a reasonable conversation, it's time to switch and try something else.

▶

3 **Involve someone else/transfer the call.** Whether you transfer the call to a supervisor or to a colleague, the customer has the opportunity to rethink their behaviour. When you transfer the call, tell the customer you've done all you can, and they need to speak with whoever it is who will now handle the problem. This serves notice to the customer that they cannot continue to abuse you, and that behaviour will be interrupted. Often when they go through to the second person the customer will apologise and take a different tack.

4 **End the call.** If you don't want to transfer the call or there is no one else you can involve and the customer is still out of control, then unfortunately you need to end the call. Before you end the call, remind them that you and your company want to help them and you are happy to do so if they are able to tell you about their problem in a reasonable manner. Let them know that you and your company are committed to helping them and that staff are advised to discontinue abusive conversations. Tell them you would be happy to talk to them again if they want to get in contact and then end the call.

5 **Protect yourself.** Remember, the customer's behaviour has nothing to do with you, so don't take it personally. They have given in to their fight response and so they are not being rational and the behaviour should not be taken personally.

Customers or criminals?

I will never forget the experience I had in a restaurant with a group of friends. It was a brand new wine bar that was attached to another restaurant where we had been regular customers over a few years and had enjoyed some really pleasant evenings. We thought it would be nice to support this new venture and tried it out deciding to invite some friends to join us. We realised when we got there that it was managed and run by someone new and, although connected to the other restaurant, it was very different. The service didn't start well; we were made to feel uncomfortable from the start. It was almost like we were under suspicion. My husband ordered a steak and asked for it to be medium to well done. It then arrived very rare and because he really can't eat it like that he politely asked for it to be cooked a bit more. The server then said 'I hope you aren't expecting a free meal' and then took the steak away. We were made to feel in that moment like criminals, out for whatever we could get; it was so unjust; we were regular customers of the other restaurant and had never sent anything back. The steak came back totally incinerated and inedible. By this time I think my husband had totally succumbed to his fight response and got very angry. The manager then came out and went on to accuse us of trying to get a free meal, telling us we were no longer welcome in his restaurant. We were made to leave and were slow hand clapped out by the staff and some of the customers. It was one of the most humiliating experiences of my life and all because my husband wanted a steak cooked the way he likes it!

This example highlights that if customers are looked at through the wrong filter, they can feel a lack of trust or they feel accused or blamed. Customer service departments talk a lot about gaining a customer's trust and creating strategies for doing this but how can we expect customers to trust us if we don't trust them? If you treat people like criminals, they start to behave like criminals.

> The chief lesson I have learned in a long life is that the only way to make a man trustworthy is to trust him; and the surest way to make him untrustworthy is to distrust him and show your distrust.
>
> Henry L. Stimson (US politician, 1867–1950)

Examples of a lack of trust

- **'Please can you put your complaint in writing.'** = 'We don't believe you and you won't put it in writing because you know you are lying.'

- **'Did you get the name of the person you dealt with?'** = 'You didn't really speak to anyone did you, go on admit it.'

- **'Leave it with us we will look into it'** = 'We will find out you're lying don't you worry.'

- **'Do you have the original packaging/receipt?'** = 'You didn't buy that here did you?'

- **'Did you wash it at the right temperature?'** = 'You didn't read the instructions and washed it too hot didn't you and now you want to blame us.'

- **'Sorry you can only take four garments at once into the changing rooms.'** = 'You could be a potential shop lifter.'

These are just a few examples and we hear them all the time ourselves. Do your best to avoid them, otherwise you may find you have to use the strategies on how to deal with abusive customers more than you want to.

Ways to build trust

● Give customers the benefit of the doubt.

● Listen to them and take notes.

● Don't base every experience with customers on the 3% of professional complainers.

● Do what you say you will do.

● Deal with customers immediately; don't pass them round.

● Be transparent.

● Involve the customers.

brilliant dos and don'ts

Handling complaints

Do

✔ Take all complaints seriously and make this clear to the customer.

✔ Deal with them straight away. Remember 95% of customers will return if their complaint is resolved well instantly. Also, research shows that customers will accept less in terms of compensation if the complaint is dealt with straight away. The more they wait, the more time they feel they have invested in it, and the more they want to be compensated for this.

✔ Offer compensation if something has gone wrong. The icing on the cake for any customer, once they have been dealt with brilliantly, is feeling valued in the form of discount, refunds, vouchers and any sort of extras. If you do this, they will be more likely to return, and in the life cycle of a customer they will pay you back over and over again with future business and word-of-mouth recommendations.

✔ Go beyond the normal service recovery. See if you can surprise and delight your customer as they did when I was in the

▶

restaurant in Malaysia. This is one of the best times to wow your customers and turn them into loyal advocates that will sell your business for you.

✔ Check with the customer that they are satisfied and ask for feedback; use this as another opportunity to thank them.

✔ Always be polite, friendly and flexible. These are the basic behaviours and will be expected. When a customer is treated with dignity, they have a feeling of fairness – very important when complaining.

✔ Be the customer's friend. Show, through your tone of voice, choice of words and general attitude that you are on their side.

Don't

✘ Tell a customer they are wrong; this will cause the customer to want to go into battle with you. Let go of wanting to be right; focus on the most important thing to move the customer back to the good-feeling place.

✘ Argue with a customer. You can never win an argument with your customers. Certainly, you can prove your point and even have the last word; you may even be right, but it's unlikely that you'd be able to change the customer's mind by arguing.

✘ Speak with an authoritative tone as if you have to prove the customer wrong. Even when the customer is wrong, this is not an appropriate response, as it makes the customer defensive.

✘ Say: 'We would never do that'. Try instead: 'Tell me more about that.'

✘ Be unrealistic in anything you promise (a twice disappointed customer is not a pretty sight!), especially if it is someone else who will have to fulfil your promise. If necessary, check that what you are promising is possible. If the solution cannot be delivered immediately, keep the customer informed of progress.

✘ Abandon the customer. Never leave them waiting unattended (especially if they are on the telephone); it just makes them angrier.

Email warning

By its very nature, email is not the best way to deal with a complaint. It's a great way to back up what you may have agreed, face to face or by phone, but dealing with a complaint by email is like dumping someone by text. It is also open to misinterpretation and if you are not careful, because it is at the finger tips of possible disgruntled customers, it could be all over the Internet in a powerful blog within minutes. If you are worried about a possible confrontation with

> dealing with a complaint by email is like dumping someone by text

a customer or you know that you or the company is responsible for causing a complaint, it will be very tempting to send an email. This is a passive response: you are hiding! Don't do it! Be brave. Pick up the phone or go and see them. It will save you time in the end and it will save your customers.

Sometimes we have no choice but to reply by email because the complaint has come in by email and there is no other way to contact the customer. Follow these basic steps to make the interaction positive.

- **Respond as soon as possible.** The average response time to an email complaint is two to four days; this is not acceptable to the customer as they want some sort of reply within hours.
- **Read the customer's email very carefully.** Just as it is important to seek to understand a customer face to face or on the phone, it is equally if not more important to understand all of the issues in a customer's email because it is there in black and white. There are no distractions or reasons why you will not have heard them. One of the things customers get most frustrated about when they get a reply to an email complaint is that all of their issues or questions have not been addressed. This is usually because there is a human tendency to stop at the first problem and

then skim over the rest. Take the time to really understand all of the issues.

brilliant tip

Cut and paste the customer's email into your reply and then work through each part of it chunk by chunk so that every bit of it is addressed. You can also use their words in your reply which shows you have read their email. Once completed you can delete their part.

- **Start with thank you.** Often we start an email with something like 'Further to your email dated...' Why do we do that? We wouldn't do it if we were talking to the customer. Don't waste words; get straight to restoring the confidence of your customer with something they want to read.

brilliant example

'Thank you for your email. We really appreciate all of the feedback we receive from our customers...'

'Thank you for taking the time to email us about...'

- **Apologise.** Yes, even if it is in writing, an apology does not have to be admission of guilt or of placing blame. The point of it is to show that you care and have empathy for the customer and to regain goodwill. Use previous tips on ways to apologise without admitting liability.

- **Explain.** Customers will always appreciate you taking time to explain why the problem occurred and it is more likely to be understood if it is in writing and, again, this is about re-establishing trust.

- **Compensate.** Don't hold back when it comes to compensating customers. Your reward will be increased customer satisfaction, loyalty and recommendations. If you can't solve the problem straight away, keep them informed.
- **Proof your email.** Check, check and check again. Any mistakes and you will look sloppy and unprofessional. Imagine seeing the email on an Internet blog. How would it look? Would you be 100% happy with it? Get a second opinion if you have any doubts at all.

Empowering staff is more than giving permission

If you manage a customer service team or are the owner of a business, complaint-handling is often an area that people are least confident about. Customer-facing staff will need more support in this area than any other. There is no point encouraging customers to complain and then not training or supporting your team to deal with them. Listen in to their calls and coach them on a regular basis to build their confidence. Appreciate the team and find ways to reward them for successfully handling complaints. Listen to them because they will be the voice of the customer.

How quickly a customer's complaint is resolved is one of the key factors in whether they will do business with you again and then go on to be your advocate. If front-line staff are empowered to settle complaints, they will save you time and money as well as reducing customer frustration.

brilliant example

A great example of this is Stena Line. Stena has empowered its staff to service recover up to the value of 1,000 euros, and this has had a dramatic effect on how they feel about handling complaints. They are more in control, and even though complaints can affect self-esteem, the customer service team members I have worked with at Stena now feel they ▶

enjoy their jobs more. They told me that when they inform customers that they will sort their problem out, it gives them a real sense of belief and conviction because they know that whatever they promise their customers they will be able to deliver, and customers have really picked up on this.

Give staff three key things:

1 The responsibility for effectively handling customer complaints.

2 Enough empowerment to make decisions they consider necessary to reach that goal (within certain boundaries).

3 A framework of action or procedure to guide them throughout the process so as to achieve complaint-management consistency across the organisation.

brilliant recap

- Remind yourself and any customer-facing staff on your team of why handling customers' complaints brilliantly is one of the best ways to develop new business.

- Understand your fight and flight responses and use strategies to minimise the effects.

- Understand your personal default position and how it manifests itself so you can remain assertive.

- Use the steps of:

  1 Acknowledge anger.

  2 Let the anger run out of steam.

  3 Appreciate and apologise.

  4 Provide an explanation.

  5 Seek to understand.

  6 Take responsibility.

- Avoid blocking language and use building language.

- End calls with abusive customers if all else fails.

- Build trust from your customers by trusting them; give them the benefit of the doubt.

- Use email carefully and remember that it should be a reflection of what you would do if you were talking to the customer.

- Managers need to empower their customer service people to take responsibility.

CHAPTER 7

How to say 'no' and still keep the customer

W e have spent a lot of time looking at ways to please customers; saying yes to them definitely helps to keep them on the correct side of the emotional scale. On the whole, everyone hates being told 'no'; from a very early age we are programmed not to want to hear it. Our parents told us 'no' all the time and it usually meant we couldn't have something delicious or do something we thought was fun, so it has a negative feeling to it from the start. We associate 'no' with disappointment or with letting someone down. For those of us who want to please, saying no can also be really difficult. Probably the last time I felt really

> we associate 'no' with disappointment or with letting someone down

comfortable saying 'no' was when I was two years old; I am driven by pleasing people and it goes against every bone in my body to say this simple two-letter word.

Of course, it is better to say 'yes' to customers and to avoid the hard 'no' because there are better ways to tell a customer you can't help them than just saying an outright no – it certainly isn't up there with the most memorable positive wow moment. However, we can take this too far if we never turn down a customer. For example, sometimes we need to say no when something is not in the best interest of the customer. I remember taking my daughter and her friend to Alton Towers, and my daughter was just at the age where she wanted to go on all the scary rides, but she was small for her age. Her friend, although the same age, was a couple of inches taller. My daughter, ever resourceful, put on a pair of wedge heels which gave her a couple of inches of height. At the first roller coaster she was so excited, eyes shining, flushed with excitement. They both approached the measurement stick and her friend was fine and was passed to go on the ride. My daughter, however, even with her extra inches was just below the scale. The assistant told her no very nicely, although she begged the assistant to let her on. I have to say my daughter is one of the most persuasive people I have ever met but the assistant stuck firmly to a gentle no, explaining how the ride was extremely dangerous if you weren't the right height. I hate seeing my children disappointed but I had so much respect for the assistant's concern for my daughter's feelings, but more importantly for her safety. So much so that I have always felt good about taking my children to Alton Towers and now my daughter is 19, she is definitely one of their best customers. The point I am making is this: there are times when we have to refuse our customers for lots of really good reasons, but how we do this is the key to keeping or losing their goodwill and possibly their business. In this chapter we are going to look at how to make it easier to say no as well as some tips on how to say it in ways that don't only limit the damage done but actually still delight your customers.

---

brilliant example

When you have to say no, find a way to turn it into a wow moment. At Disney, if a child waits in line for a ride only to find he is not tall enough for the ride, they are presented with a certificate that allows the child and the family to go immediately to the front of the line when the child is tall enough – a potentially bad moment turned into a wow moment.

When 'no' is OK

● **When you can't do it justice**. None of us want to turn business away but if we use our integrity and advise a customer that they could get a better service or product from somewhere else it really helps to build trust. A foundation of brilliant service is to give your customers what they want but do it in a way that works for your business. That means it should be something you are in business to do. Ideally, it should be something your company does better than any other.

brilliant example

I was asked to do some training for a very large drinks manufacturer; this was a new prospect and they don't come along every day, especially one this big. The course the business wanted us to deliver was on something we didn't have much experience of; we could have done it but it wouldn't have been something we could excel at. I really wanted to say yes to the business but also felt it would not be right for them and ultimately us. I said no and made a suggestion about a company that could offer them what they wanted. In the course of this conversation other key training needs emerged and I was able to sow some seeds about our offering concerning these. A month later they called me to talk about these needs and we went on to deliver a lot of training with them. Later I asked my contact why they chose us and he told me it was because we were honest. He felt if we were willing to turn work down that we weren't suited for, it gave him confidence when we were prepared to put forward our ideas about what we did go on to deliver.

This is a great example of how saying no can be the best thing you ever do to develop a relationship. If you look after regular customers and manage long-term relationships, saying yes to a customer when it's not right for them might get you business right now but it could damage the long-term potential of the account. Trying to do everything which every customer (or potential customer) asks of you can cause problems. Saying 'yes' to every request will sap your resources and drain your profits. You'll wind up doing things you're not equipped to do. You'll spend too much time learning and not enough time earning.

- **When you have to reject an idea**. If a customer makes a suggestion about your business which is not viable for you it is important to be honest, but reject the idea and not the person. A customer would rather get an honest no straight away than be left dangling.

- **It is the law**. Sometimes you're asked to do something and agreeing to do it would break the law. This one is simple. Most customers should be comfortable with the reason.

- **It's unethical**. This can be very sensitive. But never do anything that makes you feel uncomfortable or that you wouldn't want the world to know about. Be professional and diplomatic, but stand your ground.

- **It is company policy**. This one is really tricky. There is nothing I hate more than someone telling me that, due to their company policy, they won't be able to do this or that. However, it does depend on what the company policy is for. Is it for the benefit of the customer, i.e. safety issues, or is it to control the customer, i.e. we can't take the bacon out of your cheese burger?

- **When saying no is better than yes**. Customers can often get stuck in their buying habits and making different suggestions can really benefit them. Substitution is a viable alternative to many situations. Sometimes it may be obvious, while at other times you may have to take a creative approach. With the right attitude, you may find that saying 'no' is an opportunity to show how good you are.

- **Out of stock**. For whatever reason we have run out or sold out of something, so it is no longer available. A customer will have a lot more respect for you if you are honest and tell them.

- **Can't meet that deadline.** Customers will have a lot more respect for you if you are honest and realistic about delivery times or meeting deadlines, even if the information is not what they want to hear. If you say yes and then you can't keep your promise, you will lose a customer. Though turning down clients may well be one of the hardest things anyone has to do, you have to be true to yourself and have the strength to say no when it's appropriate. Never let a customer pressure you into accepting a job under terms and conditions you know you can't handle.

Understanding the blow from 'no'!

Every customer experience is full of emotion and hearing the word 'no' is a really crucial moment. We need to understand the needs of our customers if we are to make these moments positive or even wows. We can't always give customers what they ask for and they don't expect us to, but what they do want – and don't often ask for – is to be treated fairly. The following are basic customer needs:

- **To be heard and given a say.** This is sometimes all a customer really wants, even if you know you won't be able to meet their demands. Avoid the urge to interrupt them. Listen to them; take them seriously, and ask questions. That way, when you have to say no, they feel that you genuinely care and would do something if you could. Also, if you hear them, they are more likely to hear you.

- **To be treated with respect.** The most basic of all human needs, it starts with politeness and courtesy and, if appropriate, being friendly and warm.

- **To be let down gently.** No matter the reason for

the no, be careful not to bruise egos, and be aware of disappointment.

- **To feel important**. Listening will help with this; use their name; appreciate and thank them. Let them know it was OK to ask and you are always pleased to hear from them.

- **To have their pride intact**. Hearing 'no' can make us feel stupid for asking in the first place. We need to feel we can ask again and not be embarrassed.

- **Empathy and understanding**. Do everything you can to understand their point of view without criticism and judgement.

- **Reasons**. Most customers will accept a reasonable explanation, so take the time to explain why you have to say no.

- **Honesty**. Customers prefer you to be clear and honest even if it is not the news they want. Be definite in your language, for example, 'I don't think we can do that' still suggests you might be able to and can be confusing and irritating to the customer.

- **Flexibility and alternatives**. A customer wants 'no and...'; they want to know that there are other options and that you will help them. If you are willing to negotiate, let them know.

- **Control**. Customers need to feel they have an impact on the way things turn out, so find ways to involve the customer in the outcome.

- **Treated as an individual**. This goes back to personality types and different behavioural types have specific individual needs to add to these.

☼ brilliant tips

Saying no to different personality types

- The red. Pay particular attention to their ego. Status is very important to a red, so if they have put forward an idea, for example, and you can't use it, you need to leave them with their pride intact. They also prefer straight talking and honesty, so if you are a feeler (green or yellow), be careful not to irritate them with too much fluffy speak. Be direct and they will appreciate it.

- The blue. They will want clear and detailed reasons behind the 'no'. They want logical arguments and not too much emotion. Don't expect much back from them in terms of reassurance so, again, if you are a feeler, don't take this personally.

- The yellow. Sensitivity and warmth are really important. Be aware of their feelings (if you are a thinker, logic and reason is less important here than empathy and understanding). Try to end with something positive to cheer them up.

- The green. They will feel for you more than anything. They will be concerned and empathic to how you are feeling about delivering a difficult message. They will forgive you anything if you show them all of the emotional sensitivity they show you.

Using Y.E.S. to say 'no'

This is a simple acronym that will help you to remember the key techniques for saying no and still keep the goodwill of the customer:

YOU – give a bit of you! Create a connection, anything you can do to show that you are understanding, caring and appreciative. Use statements like 'I appreciate this is not what you want to hear'; 'I understand this is disappointing'; 'I am sorry that we can't get you absolutely what you want this time'. Make sure your vocal tone and body language match the meaning of your words and be careful not to use any blocking language.

EXPLAIN – give the reasons why you are saying no. Be honest and absolute. If you can blame it on a third party, they are more likely to accept it, e.g. 'We don't have any size 14s available at the moment. Because of this terrible weather, we haven't had our normal delivery in'.

SOLUTION – tell the customer what you can do, or ask what else might be of help. This is your opportunity to really wow them, e.g. 'I know we do have quite a few size 14s in other dresses that I am sure will suit you and your needs. If you want to go into the changing rooms I will bring them for you to try on'. Offer alternatives: if you can't meet their deadline or supply a product they are looking for and you understand the basis of what they are looking for, offer them an alternative. This is also an opportunity to really wow your customer if you can go the extra mile like the example below.

---

brilliant example

Back to our favourite Brazilian restaurant, Las Iguanas for another wow. We had enjoyed a lovely meal and as usual were asked if we wanted dessert. Taking the menus, my son and two daughters picked something with my husband refusing; Alejandra Friess, Deputy Manager asked why – was he on a diet? He said that he really fancied toffee sticky pudding and custard and being a Brazilian restaurant, they didn't do that sort of dessert! He had a little joke with her and she went off to organise our desserts.

Ten minutes later she came back to say the desserts were slightly delayed but they would be with us shortly. They arrived five minutes later and to our total amazement they brought out a dish of sticky toffee pudding and custard for my husband who was absolutely delighted. We later discovered they had sent a member of staff to the supermarket to buy one of their special puddings. To top it all, they didn't charge for it. We have told so many people about this wow moment and still refer back to it whenever we visit the restaurant. Our emotional scale with this restaurant is now so high that it would take a lot to put us off. They would probably have to literally throw food at us for us not to have a good feeling about it.

This example shows that if we create real wow moments with our customers and move them right up the emotional scale to delighted, not only do they keep coming back, they recommend you to everyone and they will also forgive you lots; the emotional bank account is full.

The brick wall 'no'!

If you want to upset and lose your customers then nothing will do it quicker than becoming a brick wall between the customer and what they want. Saying 'no' is uncomfortable and tricky anyway, so saying it without any empathy or any desire to help is a sure way to infuriate your customer.

What does the brick wall 'no' look or sound like?

- 'I can't help with that; it's company policy.'
- 'Have you read our terms and conditions?'
- 'It's not my job to deal with that.'
- 'I have no idea; I can't help you.'
- 'I am not allowed to do that.'
- A blank stare.
- Head down, no eye contact.
- Looking away.

⚡ brilliant example

My daughter uses the local buses a lot, and I don't know what it is about bus drivers, but many of them don't see passengers as customers. She was waiting at the bus stop and because it was raining she was inside the shelter. She saw the bus coming and it was travelling really fast, because she was inside, she had to jump out to stop it. The bus driver then gave her a really hard time because he had been forced to stop quickly (even though he had probably been going too fast); he was rude and attacked her personally. She then tried to give him a £10 note for her fare; he pointed to a sign that said they didn't take £20 notes and said he didn't have any change and she would have to get off. She started to argue with him that she had a £10 note and he couldn't just throw her off. He then threatened to physically throw her off, so she had no choice but to walk home in the rain.

This is a great example of a brick wall no and if I ever meet that bus driver I will thank him for finally giving my daughter enough of an incentive to learn to drive. You can probably think of several different options for that scenario. With a bit of flexibility and empathy it would have been a very different experience for my daughter.

☀ brilliant tip

Brainstorm as many things as you can think of that would contribute to a brick wall 'no' and things that would drive your customers mad (if you are part of a team do it together). It will make you smile and, although you might think some of the things would never happen, they act as a useful reminder of what not to do.

I wish I never had to say no to my customers, as being a yellow personality I am by nature, a pleaser and want to be liked; saying yes comes easily to me; saying no, I am still working on. I would rather sell to a brand new customer that I don't know than negotiate with one I have a long-term relationship with because I know that the negotiation will necessitate saying no. It takes practise and confidence to use the techniques in this chapter but I have found that the more I use them, the better the relationship I have with my customers. There is more respect and it feels more like a partnership. I also view saying no through a more positive filter. I don't approach it with the same dread.

brilliant recap

- Say 'yes' whenever you can.
- A 'no' isn't always a bad thing; it can benefit a customer.
- Turning down business for the benefit of our customer builds trust and loyalty and will pay dividends in the end.
- Meet the customer's basic needs to minimise the blow of 'no'.
- Recognise and adapt to the individual needs of the different personality types.
- Use Y.E.S. to say no: You (keep it personal) Explain (be honest with the reasons) Solution (offer alternatives and be flexible).
- Look for ways to wow the customers; go the extra mile.
- Avoid the brick wall 'no'.

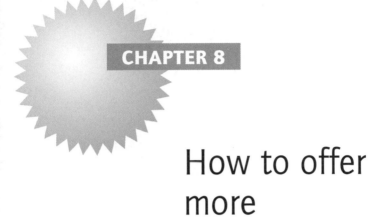

CHAPTER 8

How to offer more

Selling more and up-selling to customers when they are in a good-feeling place works for both you and the customer as long as it is done with integrity. We get more business and they get more value from the products and services they like, from businesses they trust. It's very important that we adhere to all the principles we've looked at so far in this book, and always be aware of customers' needs. There is a certain attitude, almost a stigma, attached to selling more to our current clients. It can feel a bit seedy or underhand, or perhaps we worry about spoiling the relationship by asking for more. This is the first mindset we need to change: as long as we always value and appreciate our customers and treat them with respect, there is nothing wrong with selling them more; you have earned the right to. If you have given your customers brilliant service, then they will expect and want you to offer them more.

I constantly hear customer service staff telling me they aren't salespeople and, of course, they are; they are customer facing, representing their company. They are, therefore, in the very privileged position of having the customer already on side and should see it as helping and supporting the customer as opposed to selling. Of course, salespeople also offer customer service; the two are inextricably tied together.

There are several ways to offer your customers more and here are, in my view, some the most important ones: up-selling, cross-selling, creative selling and offering new products.

brilliant definitions

Up-selling

This is when we persuade our customers to increase the value of their orders by:

● Moving 'up' to a more expensive version of what they're already considering purchasing, for example, offering a more expensive bottle of wine because it will enhance their experience of a dinner out.

● Adding to their orders with additional products or services that will enhance, or are related to the core or base product, for example, suggesting accessories to enhance an outfit.

Cross-selling

Sales of another product/service type horizontally related to what you're already considering. For instance, if you purchase a new car and the dealer encourages you to buy the company's own package to finance the purchase, that's a cross-sell.

Creative selling

Actually creating something bespoke for the customer that is specific to their needs or offering a new service to a customer that encourages them to buy more.

Offering new products

Targeting our customers with new products that we think they will be interested in.

Up-selling

This is probably the easiest way to offer our customers more; they are already buying something so they should be in a good-feeling place and buying frame of mind. It is important to do it well or it could possibly spoil the customer experience and could even take them to a bad-feeling place. It has to be viewed by the customer as being offered something that will meet their needs, or enhance what they have already bought. I have previously said how I am a big fan of Amazon; they are masters of the up-sell and it is done in a way that is informative and subtle, and you are always in control. When they suggest other books I may like, I personally love it because I love books and see it as enhanced service, not aggressive selling techniques.

brilliant example

My hairdresser, Jo, at Zig Zag in Milton Keynes, is an absolute expert at the up-sell. First of all, she is a great hairdresser and, secondly, she always gives me great service. I think the key thing is, she really listens to me, so when she suggests I buy a new shampoo or have a conditioning treatment, I listen and often say yes. I don't see that as pushy; I see it as enhancing the experience. She only ever sells me something that is right for me and if I say no, lets it go and she never puts me under pressure.

There is a skill to offering customers more by up-selling and the skill is in making the customer feel valued and understood. The number one priority is to make the customer happy because 'the only thing they never forget is how you make them feel'. If you focus on this rather than on making more money, you will make more money and you will have happy, loyal customers who will enjoy buying from you.

> the skill is in making the customer feel valued and understood

The best thing about up-selling is that it's practically effortless. Since it's done after the customer has done business with us in some way, if we have sold them a product or service, then the hardest part of the sales conversation has already been done. You've already established rapport, identified needs, given them brilliant service and they are on your side; however, it does not always happen:

The three biggest mistakes in up-selling

1 No attempt is made to up-sell.

2 The salesperson comes across as being pushy.

3 The up-selling is done in an unconvincing manner so the customer generally refuses.

How to up-sell

● Be genuinely interested in the customer and you will become very aware of the up-sell opportunities and then be positive in your approach. Assume that the customer will want the extras which you are offering.

● Avoid being pushy by asking the customer's permission before you describe the up-sell, especially if there are several benefits to describe.

● Explain the benefits of the up-sell so the customer understands the value of the extra goods or services.

brilliant definition

Benefit

A benefit satisfies a need. If there is no need, the customer will not see any reason to buy. For example, the customer tells you that they are looking for a pair of suede shoes, and once you have found them a pair they like, they ask you if they are protected from stains. You then know there is a need for stain proofing and can up-sell the appropriate product.

- Avoid asking closed questions when looking to up-sell. For example, a waiter in a restaurant might ask, 'Would you like dessert?' The answer is so often 'no'. Instead a different approach could be bringing over the menu and saying, 'We have some fantastic desserts. What do you fancy trying?'

- Focus on the customer's needs – not yours. Don't try to sell the customer something you wouldn't buy if you were in their shoes. It is totally irrelevant whether or not this purchase suits your needs. What is relevant is whether it suits the customer's. That perspective empowers you to up-sell effectively and with integrity.

brilliant tip

This is so obvious but it is so important: after any transaction with a customer ask, 'Is there anything else I can help you with today?' One of my customers, Carlsberg, has added this to its phone calls and it is already making a difference.

- If it is possible, demonstrate the product you want to up-sell or get the customer to try it on while they are on location. My hairdresser got me to try a hair wax and, once again, I was sold.

- Up-sell related products as a package deal. Again, a good example would be to sell a shampoo and conditioner together at a special rate and with the benefit that they work well together.

- Your product knowledge can really help to up-sell. I was impressed by a salesperson at the cruise company I work for because they were expert at up-selling an inside stateroom to a balcony room even though they were significantly more expensive. They were able to do it because their product knowledge was excellent and they were able to sell the improved experience for the customer. So the customer got a more memorable holiday and the company got a higher value sale.

● Enjoy the up-selling. Be passionate about your products and services and believe they will enhance your customers' experience. These days, customers don't want to be manipulated into buying. They want to interact with people who are genuinely interested in helping, who know their stuff and enjoy their work.

brilliant tip

If you are involved in business to business, when it comes to up-selling, relationships are everything. Take the time to build rapport with your customers. Understand what is important to them, not just the business, and listen to them. They will then trust you more when you make suggestions that involve up-selling.

Cross-selling

The techniques described above to improve up-selling also apply to cross-selling, although cross-selling is a little more difficult because you are not selling the same but a better product or even extras. You are selling a completely different product whose relevance the customer might not always see. Try these cross-selling tips:

● If you have established relationships with customers, spend three times as much time with them as you do chasing new customers. Relationships require maintenance. Take time and seek out other people you can sell to within your customer account.

● Ask questions that are customer focused. Get customers talking about their issues and concerns as they relate to your products and services. Listen carefully and you will then find that you can cross-sell where you are solving problems and helping your customer.

● Don't use your relationships as an opportunity to show off how much you know about your products and services if it is not relevant to your customers; you will come across as pushy or desperate and the customer will lose faith in you.

● Many cross-selling opportunities arise naturally. If you are selling tennis racquets, for example, you can also offer a bag, balls, lessons and accessories. To gain the extra sale, you might simply have to mention that the other products or services are available.

Creative selling

This is where you can really wow your valuable established customers. The selling changes from giving them what they want to creating new solutions to needs they didn't even know they had, or solving problems they didn't think could be solved. This is where you become a 'Trusted Adviser' and the relationship moves to a different level. I created a completely new workshop for one of my customers recently because I had noticed a need in the people I had been training. Not only were they surprised and delighted, but they went on to give me a lot of training days delivering this workshop and it has made a significant difference to their business. Being able to offer more to your customers comes from a trusting relationship over a period of time, but it doesn't always have to be a big thing; it could be that you order something in for a customer who mentions that they like trying new products.

> being able to offer more to your customers comes from a trusting relationship

If you are involved in business to business, then coming up with ideas could actually develop your customers' business to the point where they will not only be grateful to you but they will start to see you as a partner and then would be very unlikely to go anywhere else.

🔆 **brilliant** example

One of the best initiatives I have seen recently, which combines offering customers a brilliant service as well as more opportunity to promote business, is a company called Steljes which specialises in technology like interactive SMART boards. The company sells through re-sellers and has created a Sales Academy which is offered free of charge to all its customers. This has allowed the re-sellers to train their salespeople, also giving Steljes an opportunity to demonstrate its products; it is definitely a win–win. The re-sellers get free training and are more knowledgeable about Steljes' products, and Steljes has more goodwill and has managed to highlight its products against those of the competition – a very creative approach to offering the customer more.

Creative selling is a continuous process of letting the prospect know that his/her welfare is very important to you. It feels more like giving an excellent service than selling, although you will increase your business. No matter what you sell, you must be less concerned with the product than you are with the customer. Forget about the increased sales and focus on solving customers' problems and fulfilling their needs or desires.

✖ **brilliant** dos and don'ts

Do

✔ Know your product. The better you know the product, the better you can relay its benefits and engage the prospect in it. This also frees you up to be more creative with what you have to offer.

✔ Know the markets for your product. Are there any new uses for it? Are you selling to the right demographics?

✔ Know your customers. Are you filling the customers' needs? This is the ultimate in relationship building.

✔ Look for ideas that would solve a customer's problem or meet a need. Being creative suggests that we need to create something, so look for the opportunities. Brainstorm ideas with colleagues and even the customers themselves.

Don't

✘ Approach the opportunity with any doubt; the customer will pick up on it. If you respect your customer, your offering will be totally right for them so believe in it and see it as another way of delighting your customer.

✘ Prejudge your ideas – put them in front of the customer and let them decide if they are valuable or not.

Selling new products

Who better to try your new products than customers who already trust you? If you have given them brilliant customer service at all levels, they'll be happy to take the risk on something new and recommend you to others.

brilliant tips

● Create a buzz around your new products by offering them to your current customers first; reward them for their loyalty by offering them something special for trying out your new products.

● Involve them in the new products if you can. The cruise company I work for invites its most valued customers along to ship launches so they are the first to experience a new ship;

▶

they feel appreciated and special and are always the first to sign up to try the new itinerary. Ask customers to test new services or products at a reduced rate and then seek feedback.

● It sounds obvious but don't forget to inform your customers of what is new. Send out emails; create point-of-sale materials to highlight and create attention; send out newsletters or, if you are small enough, call them and tell them. They can't buy the new products or use them if they don't know about them.

● Maintaining relationships with your customers is crucial if you want to sell them new products or services. They might have had a great experience with you once but customers soon forget, so find ways to keep in regular contact. I am a big Arsenal fan and they are brilliant at maintaining contact throughout the season so that when they have something new to offer or it is time to renew season tickets it seems like part of the contact rather than a sales pitch. They do it by email, post, and they send out birthday cards as well.

● If you look after only a few customers, create customer profiles for them so that you will immediately know when new things come out whether they would be interested or how to put the ideas across.

Selling or service

Whether you are in sales or service, they overlap. It's all about giving the customer what they want so they stay in the good-feeling place and want to do business again. If you don't look after your customers, you'll find it very hard to offer them more because they won't want to listen to you and they won't trust you. The gym that I spent some time in while writing this book is constantly marketing to me but I don't open the emails or look at the flyers that come through by post because I am unhappy with the gym. The brilliant service must come first and then it's not a crime to offer and sell more; this is good business and what your customers expect.

Note to managers and business owners

Offering current customers more is so much easier than finding new customers, and because they already buy from you, it's much easier to get them to listen to new proposals. Often employees are nervous about selling and feel it will damage their relationships with their customers. They feel uncomfortable about the word selling because sales has a bad reputation in the UK; we see salespeople as aggressive and pushy. Good selling is actually part of brilliant service but staff will need training if they are to use any of the techniques suggested in this chapter. This will give them confidence and belief in what they are doing.

> offering current customers more is so much easier than finding new customers

brilliant recap

● You have to deliver brilliant customer service if you want to offer your customers more; they won't be in the right emotional place otherwise and will dismiss any attempts to market and sell to them.

● Always offer more with integrity; don't offer customers things that are not relevant or don't suit their needs.

● Offer more through up-selling, cross-selling, creative selling and offering new products.

● Service and selling complement each other. It is not a crime to sell to our valued customers if we have genuinely valued them; they expect and want it.

·

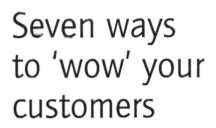

CHAPTER 9

Seven ways
to 'wow' your
customers

Everything in this book has been about giving the customer 'wow' experiences. In this chapter we bring them all together under a more generic banner. If you were to adopt any of the seven wows, you would be offering the customer something special and brilliant. There are ways to wow that might not suit you or your business but there will be at least one that will resonate and, of course, they do overlap and feed into each other. The examples are my own and demonstrate how you can have amazing positive experiences as a customer in different ways. Also, there could be more than seven ways to wow your customers, and if you have another one or have something that is completely unique to you or your business, that's fantastic.

1 The personal touch

This is all about the human connection. It's the warm smile as you approach a reception desk. It's having your name or your personal needs remembered. It's someone who is genuinely interested in you and what you have to say. It's the customer service person who offers you some genuine empathy when things have gone wrong for you. When you walk away from this type of 'wow', you feel good about yourself; you feel valued, liked and appreciated. It's almost like having a bit of magic fairy dust sprinkled on you; you can't help smiling. This is not about being polite – friendly customers expect that. This is about being authentic and genuine and making the customer feel like they are the most important person in your world at that particular moment. Anyone can create this wow – customer-facing staff, managers, and owners of businesses – and the best thing of all … it's free!

brilliant example

I was delighted to receive an invitation for the launch of one of my customer's brand new ships recently. We spent a weekend in luxury on board a truly stunning ship. We were definitely in a good-feeling place and the thing that stuck in my mind more than anything was the very personal service we had at one of the bars. On the first night the bartender asked us our names and what we wanted to drink and then spent just five minutes really connecting with us. We had our drinks and then went to dinner. The service in the bar was excellent but the real wow came the next night when we walked in. The only way I can describe the first impressions was that her face lit up when she saw us and greeted us by saying, 'Miss Debra and Mr Peter, how are you this evening? Would you like the same as last night, a glass of white wine and a bottle of beer?' When we nodded, she said she would bring it over. We were totally wowed; there were over 2,000 people on the ship and she remembered our names and the drinks we ordered. For the rest of the weekend whenever we went into the bar we got the same brilliant service. It definitely made the trip.

There are lots of businesses that have built their reputation on using the personal touch to create wows. Disney is one such company. The top cruise lines use it as a major selling point. It is very relevant for any businesses that come into personal contact with their customers, whether face to face or on the phone.

- Think of companies that you have come across which have impressed you with their personal service. Pinpoint exactly what it was that worked.

- Study the companies you admire. Perhaps you could arrange a visit to discover more about how they do it. Stena Line visited Disney to learn more about how Disney created personal wows.

The personal touch is one of the easiest and quickest ways to create a reputation for wowing customers; however, it does need to be appropriate and right for the market, the customers and the type of contact. We have probably all had experiences of the overly enthusiastic waiter in a restaurant who – when you are trying to have a quiet, intimate meal – won't leave you alone, or the shop assistant who is too pushy and in your face. There is one cashier at the supermarket I sometimes shop in who is so over the top (even though she is completely genuine) that it's just too much, and because it feels like an invasion of privacy I always avoid her till; even if it's empty I wander around a bit longer until she is serving someone and then choose another till.

Do

✔ Have your own personal code of conduct on how you will treat your customers. If you manage a team involve them in the creation of the guidelines and find ways to reward excellence in the way they are carried out. Stena Line allow staff to nominate team members for wow awards and they can put themselves forward as well. This creates a culture of every team member being aware of the impact they have as well as having fun along the way.

✔ Make the most positive and appropriate first impression you can. Make sure you really mean it and commit to it. Latest research suggests that we have between two and seven seconds to make an impression. If customers do not like your initial impact, they will look for evidence in the rest of the interaction to prove themselves right. The personal touch starts with the first eye contact and then the smile and greeting. Vary the greeting so it does not sound repetitive or scripted; the secret is to make it unique and personal to each customer.

✔ Use the customer's name; everyone likes to hear their name.

✔ Enjoy speaking to customers; be naturally curious about them and look for ways to connect. You will find that it makes your job more enjoyable and rewarding.

✔ Look for the positive in everyone. When customers behave badly, it is because they are stressed or upset and it is not personal. I saw a man being very rude to a member of the cabin crew on a recent flight and my first thought, if I am honest, was 'what a bad person'. I got the chance to talk to him later and it turned out that he had nearly been arrested at immigration because of some mix up with his passport and then he'd had to repack all of his bags to suit the silly regulations about weight. His behaviour was still bad but it was understandable. Always give the customers the benefit of the doubt; you also always have the opportunity to improve their situation.

✔ Be a brilliant listener. Make it your mission to really work on this skill. It has more impact and power than anything else. The greatest compliment we can pay anyone is to listen to them. It's so unusual to be really listened to that it creates a wow all of its own.

✔ Find ways to develop your skills. Attend training courses and seminars. Study other people in customer service and learn from your peers. Be constantly aware of your personal impact and ask for feedback from others. If you are a manager, train your staff; soft skills are probably the hardest to perfect.

Don't

✗ Use their name so much it sounds cheesy.

✗ Ever see customers as an interruption; always give them your full attention; remember: they pay everyone's wages!

2 Be the expert

If you have expertise that will help your customers, it's like gold dust and they will come to you specifically to get it. This is where you can really make your mark and wow customers every time. The key with this one is the willingness to share your expertise; there is no point in having it and then not sharing it with your customers. There is a small wine shop in our village which is more expensive than the average off licence and the owner is not always the best communicator, but does he know his wines! He is an absolute expert and is so passionate about them that you can't help but find yourself trying different types, and it keeps us coming back. Customers are drawn to people who know their business and have a passion for it.

> customers are drawn to people who know their business and have a passion for it

brilliant example

This is one of the best examples I have had personally of an expert giving me a 'wow' customer experience. I was at yet another airport and was going to a place where getting online to retrieve my emails was going to be difficult. I had my laptop with me and spotted a mobile phone shop and thought maybe they could help me with some sort of mobile connector. I did have one but it didn't seem to work in this country. I was served by a young man who was a bit geeky and didn't give me much in terms of personal connection but he was an absolute genius with regard to ▷

computers. He refused to sell me a new connector until he had determined whether the one I already had worked or not, and when he had tried everything he proceeded to set everything up for me on a new one. I was so impressed and relieved because my knowledge of computers is limited that I wanted to hug him!

This experience has really stayed with me and I now feel a certain loyalty to this brand, even though I will never do business with that particular shop again, and the reason is that I felt looked after, was so grateful for his help and was in safe hands – all of which are powerful emotions. It's a great example of how you don't always have to be a brilliant communicator; you can connect in other ways.

Recently I was doing some coaching with the sales team at a famous cruise line and I was asked to listen in to some calls of a particular salesperson. He was making more sales than anyone else and couldn't work out why as he wasn't very dynamic. After just a few calls it was clear to me why he was doing so well: he was a total expert on cruises. He had been on many of the cruises himself and loved them so much that he was able to bring them to life for the customers and reassure them about any concerns they had. His style wasn't dynamic; his voice was lacking in emotion and he didn't do chit chat, but people rang up and asked for him personally.

brilliant tips

- If you are already an expert in your business; share it with your customers and advertise it if you can.
- If you are not an expert right now, what can you do to make yourself one? Learn about your product or service. The knock-on effect is that it becomes more interesting. I once worked in a

sound and vision department selling TVs and videos (it was a few years back) and I decided to learn about one product every day. I soon became an expert, and when customers asked me what was the difference between one model and another, I was able to advise them and I made so many sales this way and, as my wages were reliant on commission, it was one way to get an edge.

- Learn from other experts. Listen to their calls or observe them when they are talking to customers.

- Find a passion for your product or service. It's much easier to learn about something if you are enthusiastic about it yourself. I wasn't that excited about TVs and videos but I found a way in and then I became the video bore at dinner parties!

- If you manage an expert, be sure to value and appreciate them; they are worth their weight in gold.

Product and services experts are very valuable to the companies they work for, are rarely made redundant and are more likely to be appreciated and valued. Not only is being an expert valuable to your customers, it is extremely valuable to an employer.

3 Easy to do business with

One company that I do loads of business with and get amazing service from is a company with which I never have human contact and yet it is one of my favourites. Everything is done via the website and email. Amazon is a great example of a company that is easy to do business with and always leaves me in a good-feeling place every time I buy from them. I know we looked at Amazon in Chapter 3 on virtual customer service, and the point I am making here is how that business creates wow moments by simply being easy to buy from. Of course, this doesn't mean this applies only to virtual businesses as most businesses can create the same experience if they are easy to work with.

In the fast paced world we now live in we don't want things to be more difficult. Customers experience frustration, irritation, even anger, if they find things difficult, yet, it seems to be a constant thing. That's why as a company or individual you can really wow your customers by being easy to do business with.

brilliant dos and don'ts

Do

✔ Show how important it is for you to deal with customers quickly; be proactive in reacting to customers' needs.

✔ Have a look at your phone system; nothing impresses me more when I ring a call centre than to be put through to the right person quickly and easily, because these days it seems more difficult to achieve this.

✔ Take responsibility for the customer's needs. If you are not the right person to speak to, do your best to help them; take the effort out of any transfer.

✔ Get rid of procedures, systems, rules or terms and conditions that make it difficult for customers. Airlines with their current, problematic policies on baggage are driving a lot of customers mad and, from my own personal experience, they are turning to airlines which are more flexible and less controlling, even if a little more expensive.

Don't

✘ Keep customers waiting. Deal with them straight away if possible and keep queues to a minimum, otherwise they will give up and go somewhere else.

✘ Make it difficult for customers to get information; they will go somewhere where it is easier.

✘ Get defensive about complaints. If customers find it difficult to complain, they won't and you lose customers. It's hard to believe but by encouraging and appreciating complaints you can create a wow experience. It makes you less risky to deal with and customers have peace of mind thus making their life easier.

✗ Do things for your ease if they make it difficult for the customer. For example, as I write this, I am in a hotel and they have just knocked on my door at 8.00 a.m. on a Saturday morning to ask me if I am going to breakfast as they want to get all the rooms cleaned early today because they have a large group arriving later. This suits the hotel, but it doesn't suit me.

In this modern world of stresses and strains and a lack of time, if you can find ways to make your customers' lives easier, they will appreciate you for it and come back to you time and time again.

4 The power of yes

Customers love it when you say 'yes'. It comes back to feeling important and special, and pushes them up the emotional scale. Looking for ways to help your customers when they have a request (as long as it is reasonable) can go a long way towards the wow moment. Businesses do crazy things to customers in the name of policy and terms and conditions. A friend of mine went for breakfast in a branch of a large restaurant chain and asked for the full English breakfast but without the hash browns. She was told that she had to have them because it was a set break-fast, so when she got the food she took two hash browns off her plate and threw them away. This had two consequences: she was mildly irritated and the company was wasting food and money.

Sometimes businesses create rules that can get in the way of taking care of customers. Of course, we do need rules and guide-lines, even terms and conditions, so that there are no grey areas, but these can go too far and then be used as an excuse for being

too often we focus on one way to do something

lazy. Too often we focus on one way to do something. Maybe it's the only way we know. Maybe it's the fastest, cheapest or easiest route to helping our customer. But that doesn't make it the best.

Being flexible often doesn't cost anything. There are some great companies out there that have built their reputation and business on saying 'yes' and adding the 'wow' factor to their service.

brilliant example

While staying in a hotel with a colleague, she discovered at breakfast that the coffee was awful, totally undrinkable. The hotel was pretty awful too and the coffee 'thing' was the final straw. Later on that day, while shopping we found ourselves looking for some decent coffee, which we found. However, without a coffee machine it still didn't seem possible to get a decent cup of coffee. We then had the idea of buying some filters and somehow create a makeshift coffee maker but then we couldn't find filters anywhere. Eventually, a lovely shop assistant suggested we try the local coffee franchise, which we did and although they had filters for their own coffee they didn't sell them. We asked just to be sure and the assistant listened patiently to our story of woe about how bad the coffee was, etc. and she explained she was sorry they didn't sell coffee filters. But even despite her boss telling her not to, she gave us enough filters to last our stay in the hotel. Brilliant! My friend was delighted and has vowed to always use that coffee shop from now on.

Of course, flexibility is only possible if the front-line staff are empowered to make their own decisions. The good companies teach or train their employees on how to come up with alternatives to anything that might get in the way of taking care of the customer. For example, a restaurant/shop may be out of something. Rather than just say we're out, the member of staff should suggest alternatives. This might have to be sold to the customer but this is all part of giving them a wow moment. Or they could decide to break or bend the rules for the benefit of the customer. It's all about trust and about taking responsibility.

So we're trying to teach our employees to work around having to tell a customer anything they don't want to hear. This is about being flexible, which I discussed earlier. But now we approach it with a concept I term 'the service alternative', which is simply offering the customer an alternative that is acceptable and that may not just meet, but maybe even exceed, the original expectations. Getting there is not difficult. There are several questions to ask that will help get you the answer.

brilliant tip

When put in a situation where you are not sure whether to bend the rules and be flexible, ask yourself:

● Is what the customer wants really unreasonable?

● Is what the customer wants going to hurt the company in any way?

● Will it compromise profit?

● Is it illegal or will it cause harm to anybody? (In this instance it is always OK to say, 'No!')

● What can I give the customer that is a reasonable substitute?

● Will this substitute meet or even exceed the original expectations?

This is the thought process that creates a culture where you can say 'yes' as much as possible. It is customer focused, versus company or operations focused. Being flexible also means being willing to try new things and go the extra mile for customers.

It means being a problem solver rather than an order taker. Customers know the difference. Stay flexible as you provide solutions to your customers. They'll thank you with their loyalty.

a wow moment for a customer can also become a wow moment for you

I have found that sometimes saying yes to a customer has meant my business taking a leap forward; we become more creative and it stimulates ideas which then go on to help other customers and I look back on them as milestones for my business. So a wow moment for a customer can also become a wow moment for you.

brilliant tip

If you are a manager or business owner, teach your team to ask themselves these questions. Even better, have a meeting and create different scenarios that force a service alternative. Brainstorm them. Publish these as examples in the employee handbook as a guide and primer to how to deal with negative news from the customer.

5 Trust the customer

To be trusted is a greater compliment than to be loved.

George Macdonald

Throughout this book we've explored the idea of looking at customers through different coloured filters. Well, to pull off this wow, you have to always look through a positive filter. You have to see customers as honest and trustworthy and always expect the best of them. You cannot let isolated incidents of customers taking you for a ride get in the way. This is about never blaming the customer; it's about respecting their views and giving them the benefit of the doubt.

⚡ brilliant example

I recently bought my husband some headphones for his birthday and ended up buying two pairs because I wasn't sure which type he would like best. I actually bought them from two different shops and it was interesting to see the differing policies of each outlet and the impression they had on me. In one store they told me that if I took the headphones out of the package or they looked damaged in any way the store would not refund my money or exchange the headphones. The second store said that the headphones could be tried out and used for 14 days and if my husband didn't like them we could exchange or have a refund as the headphones were just sent away to be re-covered. It's not hard to guess which headphones went back!

One of the worst emotional experiences for most customers is being made to feel like a criminal and viewed as dishonest. We have probably all had experiences of taking goods back and feeling very uncomfortable while they are inspected to see if they have been used. Trust your customers and they will trust you and reward you with more business.

⚡ brilliant example

John Lewis and Waitrose have a fair and efficient refund policy and have just topped a poll of 14,000 shoppers, polled about their service and attitude to customers. It is one of the key reasons they are one of the only retail companies to have increased their sales during the economic downturn.

Trust, of course, is a two-way thing so you need to promote your own trustworthiness by keeping your promises and always doing what you say you are going to do. If you offer a money-back guarantee, then stick to it with no conditions; its original purpose was to give the customer security, so don't blow it when it's tested.

> ### ✦ **brilliant** dos and don'ts
>
> **Do**
>
> ✔ See the best in your customers.
> ✔ Keep your promises.
> ✔ Make your customers feel comfortable when then return goods or call in a money guarantee, etc.
>
> **Don't**
>
> ✘ Expect customers to be dishonest.
> ✘ Blame the customer; take responsibility yourself.
> ✘ Make customers feel bad for complaining or doubt their story.

6 Honesty

You might think this one is a given and that merely meeting the customers' expectations at its most basic level won't really create a wow. However, you have to go further with it to develop a reputation for yourself and your business of honesty and integrity. Only then will customers be wowed since there is no better way to build customer loyalty. Make it your policy to continually promote honest business practices, top-rated customer service and integrity. Below you will find a few simple tips to follow that provide guidance in developing credibility that can make you stand out and wow your customers.

> ### ✦ **brilliant** tips
>
> ● Be proud of the product or services being offered through the business and always be totally truthful about what you offer. This means you also need to be prepared to tell the customer if your product or services don't meet their needs and even better to actually point them in the right direction to get what they want.

- If you have influence over the way your products and services are promoted, then be clear and honest in any adverts or marketing. There is nothing worse than going to an outlet in search of a great deal promoted in the local paper, only to find that it is no longer valid or there are added requirements to take advantage of it. Customers will feel misled. Everything must be clear and to the point at all times. Remain impeccable with your word and your customers will respect you for it, and your reputation for being a company with integrity will grow.

- If you offer warranties or guarantees, make sure it is clear to customers how to take advantage of these and then stick to your word if they call them in; not only will the customers respect and trust you more, they will also recommend you because the risk is much lower.

- Encourage and welcome complaints and make this a positive experience for the customers. This will build their loyalty and promote further business because the risk of buying from you is much lower and, again, they are more likely to recommend you.

- Treat all of your customers fairly and with respect. All customers should be provided with the same deals and services, not just special customers. No one wants to feel inferior because their wallet isn't as full and it can be dangerous to make assumptions. Make every customer feel as if they are the only one in the room or on the phone that matters.

- Have your own personal policy never to talk badly of customers no matter what happens and if you are a manager or business owner, make this part of your company policy. Always talk about customers positively and with respect.

- It's really important not to bad mouth your competition in front of the customer because you could be bad mouthing their personal choice. Be positive about your competition and even recommend them if it is appropriate; this will surprise and wow your customers.

7 The element of surprise

Most of us, including our customers, live a life that is full of routine and rituals. On the whole, we are creatures of habit even in our buying habits; for example, we get used to shopping at the same supermarket because we know where everything is and we end up taking things for granted. What we used to be really impressed by no longer has the same impact. So to create brilliant moments, we have to break these habits and patterns of thought, which is where the element of surprise comes in. Get this right and you can really wow your customers.

What's amazing about the surprise wow, is that it promotes word-of-mouth recommendations. It is designed to cause a reaction and because it is something the customer is not used to or had before, it gives them something to talk about and they are more likely to tell the story to lots of people. Surprising a customer gives them a new experience and one they are likely to share with others for a long time. You may remember the story

> surprising a customer gives them a new experience and one they are likely to share

about the waitress who went out to the supermarket and bought my husband sticky toffee pudding. We must have told hundreds of people about that experience and now it has even been mentioned in this book several times – proof of the pudding!

Getting it right

When surprising our customers, the timing and the nature of the surprise makes all the difference. It's worth knowing your audience and if you know what they expect you can then look at what would surprise them. No one knows their audience as well as someone who lives with it every day. And once you know what they're expecting, it's your job to give them what they're not.

brilliant tip

If you are a manager or owner of a business, involve your team in brainstorming ideas on how to surprise your customers. Make sure you reward and appreciate them for any great ideas. Sometimes having your idea adopted is the best form of recognition.

There are lots of ways to surprise customers and below are some ideas to get you started and help stimulate your thought processes. Often you won't know how to surprise them until you are presented with an opportunity, and then it will be clear what to do. It will then depend on how much commitment and energy you give that counts. One thing to remember, there is nothing more satisfying and sure to make you feel good than doing something nice for someone and seeing the look on their face or sound of their voice. Try it and you will be surprised yourself how it makes you feel.

brilliant tips

1 One of the easiest ways to surprise customers is to give them really personal service and this is where wow number one really can overlap. Aim for lots of little things and 'major in the minors'; go for 101 little things done with the customers' interest uppermost in mind.

2 Make the effort; don't give up too easily and you will be remembered for going out of your way. You will also make a name for yourself within the business as well.

3 Surprise customers by doing something that is both personal and valuable to them. Decide what feeling you're trying to inspire (awe, joy, excitement, disbelief, horror, etc.) and then be creative about how you can deliver it. When you're doing it,

think small. Don't go for the elaborate plan. Go as small as you can because it's the little things done better than expected that create the biggest wow.

4   Show up where they don't expect it. On one very hot day I got back to my hotel to see the porters standing outside handing out bottles of ice cold water to customers as they came back to the hotel, wow!

5   Give them something different: lots of businesses offer free gifts along with a purchase. It's the coupon slipped into the bag at the register, the free makeup brush someone gets with their purchase, a trial of a new scent – the problem is these have raised customer expectations and no longer have the same impact. Think about what you could give that's different that gets them talking. You don't have to get pricey to surprise someone; you just have to deliver something they weren't expecting. Be careful about giving away branded gifts. Most customers don't like them and don't see them as valuable; what do you do with gifts like this? That's right, we normally throw them away.

6   Listen when they think you're not. The surprise wow works by giving someone something they needed at a time they weren't expecting it. I found myself with a colleague in yet another reception in yet another hotel and while collecting my key, we were chatting about the exhausting day we had just experienced and how much we were looking forward to relaxing in the bar. As we walked to the bar we were handed two glasses of sparkling wine on the house, just because we had had a hard day. We didn't realise it, but the receptionist had listened to our conversation and rung through to the bar. It was a lovely touch and now a favourite hotel.

There are lots of ways to surprise and delight your customers and the more personal they are the better. Just be aware that the surprise wow will not work if your normal service is sloppy or the customers' expectations are not being met in other areas. It will just be seen as an insincere gesture to win them over, so it is important that they are the icing on the cake. Also, if you offer brilliant service and the odd surprise, customers will give you the benefit of the doubt if anything goes wrong. The best thing of all is that not every profession is in the habit of creating memories. It's the power of the unexpected and it doesn't get much better than that.

brilliant recap

- Before you can wow your customers, you need to meet their expectations in all other areas first; you should not use them to distract from poor service.

- There are many ways to wow customers; play to your strengths and look for areas where you can make a real difference.

- Remember the seven ways to wow your customers:

  1   the personal touch;

  2   be the expert;

  3   easy to do business with;

  4   the power of 'yes';

  5   trust the customer;

  6   honesty;

  7   the element of surprise.

Conclusion

To deliver brilliant customer service, you have to like your customers. It's all about which colour filter you are viewing your customers through. When I work with some businesses, I am amazed at the way customers are talked about, often negatively and even scornfully. The one thing a customer can pick up very quickly is whether you are genuine or not and they know if they are not being valued. We all have experiences of brilliant service and poor service and yet it is challenging to be consistent. If you can create a culture in your business, or in your team, or as an individual, of wanting to understand customers' needs, appreciating their importance, you will be able to deliver brilliant service no matter what the situation.

There is no better way to grow a business than through loyal customers who keep coming back, going on to be your advocates, selling your business for you through recommendations and referrals. It costs a lot to get a customer in the first place but if you treat them well, they will repay you tenfold.

I am really looking forward to receiving brilliant customer service as direct results of you reading this book and putting into practice all the techniques. Go for it and enjoy it – it's so much more fun being brilliant!

Index